# HAUNTED
# CHARLESTON

# HAUNTED CHARLESTON

## ED MACY AND GEORDIE BUXTON

Haunted
America

Published by Haunted America
A Division of The History Press
Charleston, SC 29403
www.historypress.net

Copyright © 2004 by Ed Macy and Geordie Buxton
All rights reserved

First published 2004, Second printing 2005, Third printing 2006,
Fourth printing 2008, Fifth printing 2011, Sixth printing 2012

ISBN 978-1-5402-0358-8

Library of Congress Cataloging-in-Publication Data
Macy, Ed.
Haunted Charleston : stories from the College of Charleston, the Citadel, and the Holy
City / Ed Macy and Geordie Buxton.
p. cm.
Includes bibliographical references.
print edition ISBN 1-59629-011-0 (alk. paper)
1. Ghosts--South Carolina--Charleston. I. Buxton, Geordie. II. Title.
BF1472.U6M33 2004
133.1'09757'915--dc22
2004025575

The names of some people involved in these stories have been changed either by their
request, or because their relatives have asked us to do so.

The poem "Shadow in the Empty Eye" was previously published as "A Southern
Adolescence Recognized" in Musings of the Lowcountry, 1995; Garnet, 1995; New
Millennium Writings, 2000 and Channel Surf, 2000.

Photo Credits
page 54 Post & Courier
pages 70, 90, 108–09, 114 Laurens Smith
page 112–13 Frank Ruopoli
Other photos courtesy of the authors.

Notice: The information in this book is true and complete to the best of our knowledge. It is
offered without guarantee on the part of the authors or The History Press. The authors and
The History Press disclaim all liability in connection with the use of this book.

# CONTENTS

# CONTENTS

*To my muse. You know who you are.*

# SHADOW IN THE EMPTY EYE

*In this pale crescent moon, I see the angels cross over*
*With their ghost bombs and fresh winds, scattering*
*The heat lightening and droning clouds away*
*From my island home, steering the storms*

*Across the harbor where unheard rebel captains*
*are still murmuring below the watermark. Inside*
*its Battery sea walls, Charleston's spires grow*
*taller, and the lunatics and businessmen take shelter*

*In the shadows of the cobblestone alleys along East Bay.*
*A snowy egret, anchored in plough mud, rises*
*like a sleepy child and stretches out his wings*
*through the sharp blades of the marsh grass;*

*Above, hidden behind the mossy silhouettes*
*of Spanish oaks and the tall reviewing spires,*
*there are soft whispers of Gullah, glowing*
*in starry hints of blue and green and gold.*

*Those bright hushed voices haunt me now, and this*
*universe is falling fast like thunder to the watermark:*
*the moon has lit the egret on fire, and she blazes*
*momentarily over an unexpected flood tide.*

—Geordie Buxton

# Introduction

This book covers new territory involving Charleston's ghosts—literally and figuratively. Few of these stories have ever been published, and they take place away from the average postcard shots of the city: the moss- and ivy-strewn campus of the College of Charleston, the imposing fortress of the original Citadel, and the neighborhoods that once lay near the boundary of the city. These stories and essays are more grim and morbid than the stories that have been published previously about the Holy City's ghosts. In many cases, they are more tragic because of the age or the number of people involved. That is the face of history, and I cannot as a writer presume to make these stories more digestible. I must tell them as they happened and let the reader make his or her own decisions on how to accept them.

There is only one essential ingredient in a ghost story: death. Immediately upon discovering this, one realizes the topic at hand is inherently morbid. It is this high-speed train wreck fascination that keeps the reader or the listener attentive, alert and somewhat (hopefully) uneasy. Ghost stories exist not to fill the public's desire for morbidity or gore. They exist because these real events happened to very real people. These were living beings who died in wars, in pistol duels and in acts of God and Mother Nature. The dramatic suspense does not need to be embellished, because these things actually occurred.

Embellishment can and does thrive in ghost legends, however. These are the stories wrought from the human desire to become a slave to the storyteller. Often, but not always, these are tales of real events that have been padded or twisted to take on a whole new life. They can become part of the

# INTRODUCTION

cultural subconscious. As a storyteller, I am not opposed to ghost legends. I simply feel they should remain in their proper category, and not passed off as ghost stories.

Unfortunately, this genre has already been victim to endless stereotyping and cliché bombardments. The concept of the ghost as a chain-rattling, sheet-draped phantom is infuriatingly ingrained in our cultural heritage. The American Halloween culture did for ghosts what the Book of Genesis did for the snake: both cast their subjects in a light to be feared and even despised, when in fact there is no real justification for this.

Another element of stereotyping involves the ever-familiar "famous ghost." I once heard a carriage tour guide tell a group of gullible tourists that General Robert E. Lee haunted the Mills House Hotel on Meeting Street. Now, granted, I do not know everything that went on in Lee's personal life during his short stay at the hotel in the beginning months of the Civil War. But I can almost guarantee that nothing happened here to rival the emotion and psychic trauma the man endured years later on the battlefields of Virginia, Appomattox Courthouse or Arlington, his mansion-turned-cemetery. My point is that every city has a famous ghost. It is an epidemic we must endure, as the ghost genre gets more popular and more commercialized. People love to put the famous name to the not-so-famous ghost. Fame and notoriety sell. It's been proven.

This book contains ghost stories based on real history and specific details. There are no elements of mystery, intrigue or romance embellished to make for a more "frightening" story. Truth is stranger than fiction, meaning the natural and historical drama in these stories provides wonder. The specific details provide the almost shocking realism. Today's reader demands more than ambiguous, question-marked rhetoric, i.e.: "and some believe the ghost still haunts the manor to this day. Do you?"

There are many books that will provide readers with a false sense of mystery and adventure. The stories in these books are set in obscure, out-of-the-way locales, some of which do not even exist anymore. It may have worked in the early 1960s, but today's reader is far more jaded. They expect the details wrought from great scrutiny. John Bennett's *Doctor to the Dead*, while highly entertaining, is in a completely different genre. It focuses on cultural superstitions and orally translated folk-tales.

*Haunted Charleston* provides the significant dates, locations and names of these stories. We also range the readers' senses in describing how the ghosts are experienced. All of our settings are real, extant and can be seen by the reader upon visiting Charleston.

# INTRODUCTION

I have been asked numerous times by television producers why Charleston has so many ghosts. For the first few naïve years, my standard reply was "it's an old city that has seen a lot of death. . . ." Granted, this is true, but it could also be said for hundreds of communities on this continent. If asked today, I try to answer more philosophically. I now tell interested parties that the spirit world crystallizes around objects of familiarity. By law and common sense, Charleston has entire neighborhoods that have never changed physically. Not just the exteriors of the structures, preserved for the sake of historic importance and tourism, but even small details inside: doorknobs, light fixtures and, unfortunately in some, plumbing and electrical wiring. This city has changed dramatically in a cultural and social sense. The smell and view and placement of property, however, would look the same to a person who died two hundred years ago.

In my opinion, ghosts are a phenomenon much like fog or humidity, only harder to explain. Ghosts are images emblazoned onto spatial property because of some tragic emotional or psychological experience, or the classic "unfinished business." Not having a background in science, I cannot give any better definition, save for the following stories . . .

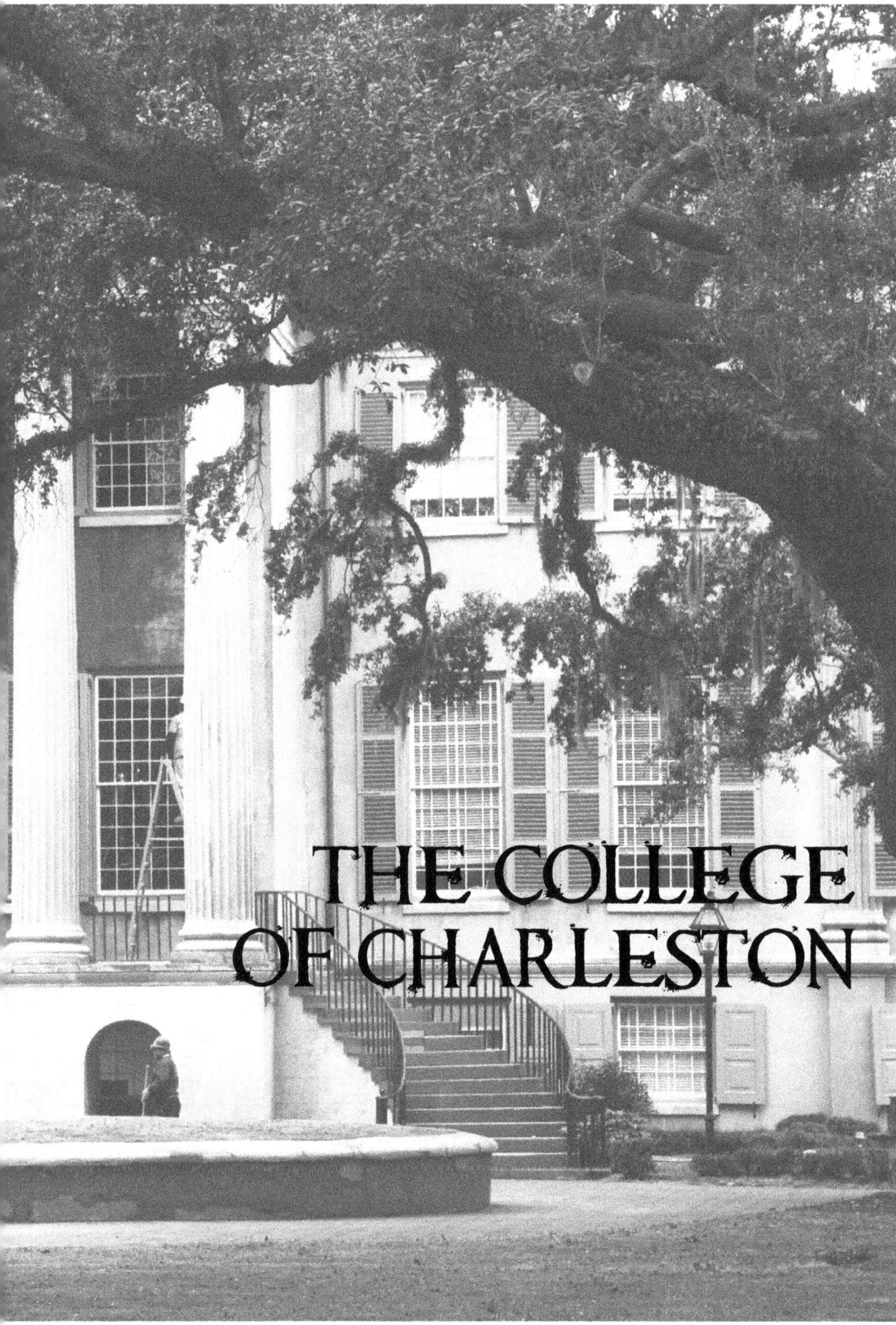
THE COLLEGE
OF CHARLESTON

# THE ORPHAN POLTERGEISTS

The poltergeists that haunt the College of Charleston's Joseph E. Berry dormitory are as mischievous as they are mysterious. This building was once the site of The Charleston Orphan House, which, in October of 1918, faced one of the greatest challenges of its time. The Spanish Influenza epidemic had infected over two hundred orphans with the flu and many were near death. Miss Lesesne, the superintendent, who was already short-handed in nursing and supplies because of the wartime decline in charitable donations, called in every staff member she could find to keep the sick children from passing away. More young lives were at stake than during the great earthquake of 1886, the diphtheria epidemic of 1908 or the starvation earlier in the century resulting in geophagia, or eating dirt.

For the children who were immune or spared from the Spanish Influenza, large open play yards were always accessible without the reviewing eye of staff disciplinarians, who were overwhelmed with tending to the sick. The frantic time was a great vacation away from the routine discipline of "The Door," or Miss Dorine Blackman.

Small in stature but big in heart, Miss Blackman was raised in the nineteenth century and spent many years in the sewing department of the orphanage before eventually becoming the superintendent after Miss Lesesne died at her post. She was given the nickname "The Door" because when matrons sent misbehaving children down to see her, Miss Dorine would hold court, like a Catholic confessional, from behind a closed door.

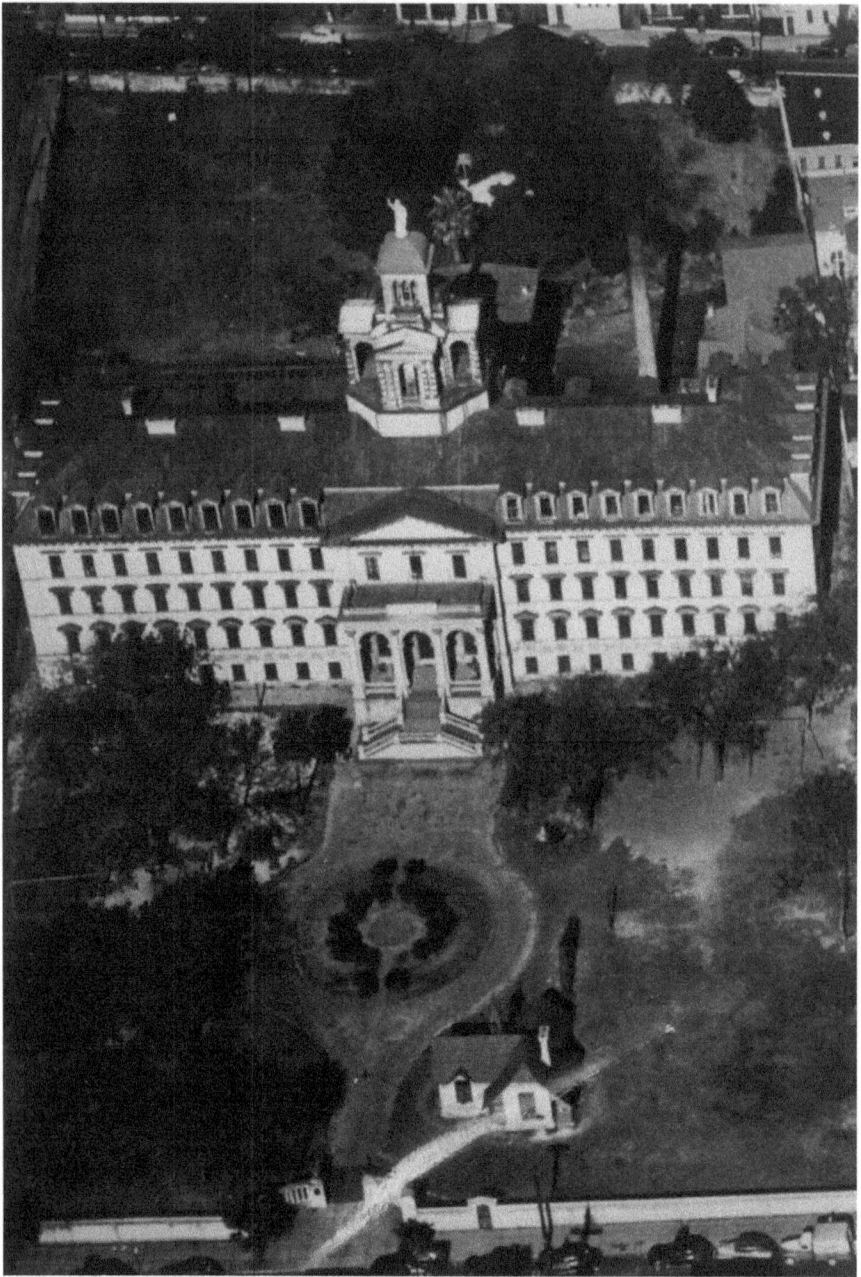

# THE COLLEGE OF CHARLESTON

Children enjoyed talking to Miss Dorine outside of her office because they could stand and look her eye to eye. However, they knew that when she said to do something that they were not to question her. But some of the older orphans did test the boundaries of their independence with subversive battles against the disciplinarian. Their confidence for revolution in the orphan house grew to rebellious heights with a wide-open, unsupervised play yard during the October of the Spanish Influenza epidemic.

Most of the revolting children's insurgency was based on a gripe over Mother Nature. The Charleston orphans had seen pictures of orphanages in the lush, green rolling hills of the Blue Ridge, with children fishing and skipping stones across flowing mountain streams. They looked at their brick, dusty city play yards and longed for a livelier setting.

Orphans took cardboard boxes from the trash to make tents in the play yards. They would crawl inside their tents and poke twigs out, make-believing they were fishing a river or roasting meat on a campfire. The staff of the orphan house became infuriated when visitors came to look at the remarkable gothic revival building and saw cardboard boxes and sticks windswept across the grounds. Whenever a child was seen digging through the trash to make a cardboard tent, he was sent to Miss Dorine. Many orphans remained hidden inside their tents once the cardboard was hastily assembled, even after their names were called out for misbehavior, forcing The Door to come to them.

In an attempt to gain ground on the short-staffed administration during the flu epidemic, the little devils made a tent and filled it with detestable liquids and solids. They snatched an oily rag from the kitchen late at night and lit it with matches. Tossing the burning rag on the cardboard, the orphans ran to a hiding spot to watch The Door come out of the building to stamp the smelly brushfire out. The plot worked in theory, providing great amusement for the insurgents, as they waited in delight for The Door. But The Door, buried in the exhausting trenches of caring for over two hundred sick children, didn't come.

The fire soon grew, leaping from tent to tent, and before the troublemakers knew what to do, the wind was pushing the fire onto the walls of the infirmary where the sick children lay lethargic in their cots. By the time the black smoke billowed into the infirmary, the city fire bell that hung just below Lady Charity's statue above the seventh floor was ringing loud and rapidly. As the disbelieving rebel children looked in panic at what they had done, The Door appeared before them.

Four children died during the October fire, according to orphan house records. There is no evidence anywhere of any substantial damage to the building itself. The orphan victims of the tragic fire most likely left this world

in their sleep, oblivious to the black smoke and fumes circling about them. Perhaps they were dreaming of a time when they would be free of the influenza in hopes they might return outside to dance and sing again in play parties.

During the evacuation of the infirmary that fateful night of 1918, one can only speculate how long it took to remove over two hundred sick children laying in comatose states. If these four orphans were left behind in the darkness of the night and thick fumes, their giddy haunting leads one to believe they left the world in peace. They seem to have returned as if they have no knowledge anything happened to them. They have jumped back up from their fall into stillness and rejoined the cycle of life, holding hands in an invisible spirit dance along the grounds of the Joe E. Berry dorm on the College of Charleston's campus.

A rash of false fire alarms went off throughout the building in the first years of its existence. Every time a sudden fire alarm rang, which was almost always in the wee hours of a quiet night, the city fire marshal and his crew would respond hastily in anticipation of an emergency. Every room would be combed for signs of smoke or fumes while students were rushed to assemble outside, more often than not in their underwear.

The Berry dorm residents were interrogated over and over for confessions. They became as vexed by the late-night fire alarms as the men and women questioning them. The fire marshal went through great lengths to catch the culprit of these false alarms by putting an invisible pixie dust on the alarm handles so that when one was pulled, he or a fire-fighting colleague could shine a black light on the suspected students' hands to reveal the mark of sin. None of the fire department's tactics revealed anything.

The fire department then turned to the college with a list of fines for every time their men and women were called down to investigate the false alarms. The message sent to the college was to either rewire the Joe E. Berry dormitory's alarm system or gain more control over the students. The college analyzed the problem and dismissed all the males from the co-ed dormitory in 1996, making it an all-female dorm in 1997, which is how it remains today.

The exile of the freshman males in the mid-1990s temporarily lessened the onslaught of false alarm outbreaks. However, a set of heated complaints from the visiting parents of prospective students as well as the current students in the dorm caused another situational firebomb that the college has not yet been able to extinguish. Students kept awake by the sounds of distant voices of small children were the first to report in the set of new disturbances in the dorm. Echoing metallic squeals and laughter in and around the building were repeatedly described as the source of the trouble. The eerie sounds were heard traveling through the halls, stairwells, air conditioning vents and under the trees on the outer brick courtyards of the Berry dorm between 2:30 and 5:00 a.m.

Visiting parents of prospective students are occasionally offered complimentary rooms in the new dorm during the annual summer break. It is a welcoming stay given by the college for visitors to experience genuine Southern hospitality before they go on a guided tour of the historic campus the following day. Many guests have never shown up for the day tours. Some of the parents have called their tour guides the next day with bellicose complaints: "Where are the parents of these children running wild in the middle of the night?"

The disembodied voices heard were generally described in interviews with those who heard them as eerie, but celebratory. In several accounts, the distant metallic inflections of rhymes permeated in circles through the air vents and around the dorm's outer walls. A few witnesses noted hearing the high-pitched chanting of a popular children's party game, "Ring Around the Rosie," a poem made popular in Kate Greenaway's 1881 book of children's rhymes *Mother Goose*:

> *Ring around the rosie*
> *A pocket full of posies*
> *Ashes, ashes*
> *We all fall down*

College guides apologized profusely to dissatisfied parents by passing on, with little success, inventive excuses to discount the spirit noises. Some believe that one of these excuses led to an extensive HVAC renovation by the Rosenblum Coe Architect firm in the summer of 2003. The most involved of the guides' explanations, for the exhausted parents who would listen, entailed the Berry dorm's metal air conditioning vents, which were said to be squeaking against the duct insulation as air whisked through, causing a high-pitched frequency that some visitors might confuse with children recreating in a nearby play yard.

As the theory about the HVAC system circulated around the campus, the false fire alarms resumed with another series of outbreaks in the all-female dormitory at the turn of the millennium. The college dorm was up to its ears in fines and complaints at the end of its first decade of existence.

In the summer of 2003, the college began the enormous HVAC renovation. A plywood wall was built around the entire building to allow the Rosenblum Coe architect firm to begin work. No visitors stayed at the Berry dorm during construction that summer. The old HVAC system was gutted out to make way for a more efficient, modern replacement and the fire alarm system was modified.

When the Berry dorm reopened for use, the strange occurrences of the false alarm outbreaks and the paranormal activity did not stop. In fact, the false alarm outbreaks increased.

In paranormal research, one major criterion for hunting down a ghost is death. Someone has to have died. The death may snap a life short with a man-made or natural disaster, as in the case of the Berry dorm haunting, or it may be slow and peaceful. A sudden exit from humanity leaves some spirits to crystallize, in one form or another, around the familiar setting of their past. In the case of the Berry dorm, the haunts are not as easy to reveal in the mischievous, invisible forms they are in.

It is believed that the child poltergeists travel in a pack or group because of the many giddy voices that are heard in circular laughter and song. The voices have been described in accounts to be as few as three and as many as seven. But to find a right number and who they might be requires excavating historical vaults and digging through the dirt of the orphanage's records.

For three American centuries, hundreds of orphans had experienced life in the Charleston Orphan House, built in 1790 directly on barracks used in America's War for Independence to house children who lost their parents in the Revolutionary War as well as French refugees displaced by the Santo Domingo slave rebellion. In 1952, the building was leveled for a Sears Roebuck building in the city council's shortsighted attempt to revitalize the area.

The windswept statue of Lady Charity, which graced the high cupola of the seven-story orphan house, a symbol of benevolent goodwill for centuries of vulnerable children of circumstance, was whipped down by cables hooked to a bulldozer, and smashed to smithereens. All that remains of one of America's finest antiquities is a city fire bell that was relocated to the Carolina Youth Development Center in North Charleston.

The city's jabberwocky plan for business development failed just a few years after the first cash register was rung. The college then moved in to renovate the empty department store for its new Lightsey Conference Center.

The concrete parking lot in front of the store, once the great walled entrance to the Charleston Orphan House grounds, was chiseled through to build the college's Joe E. Berry dormitory in the late 1980s. The new dorm opened its doors to freshman men and women in 1991. The disembodied voices of several children, lingering after one night of terror, can still be heard laughing and singing on the present-day landscape.

While a few ghosts around the historic peninsula of Charleston send out clear, chilling messages about their lives, others are more obscure and may not be aware of their own fate. The Berry dorm spirits sound cheerful, playful and oblivious that their life on earth has passed. However, in speculation, their presence seems far from angelic. If they are indeed angels, they have missed the mark on saving lives from fire time and time again. Their clumsiness is simply a reflection of the youth of the personalities involved in the haunting. The false fire alarms and the sung words heard by witnesses point to the only record of a fire in the historical time lapses of the Charleston Orphan House.

# THE SILENT MOVIE

The College of Charleston purchased the antebellum single house at 12 Glebe Street in 1966. At some point before this, one of the previous tenants had created a confusing maze inside the house. Plywood sheets had been put up over all of the doors and window transoms. There was even a well-built wall constructed in front of the staircase. The fifteen-room house had been reduced to a single-room unit.

After the purchase was final, the school sent a crew inside to evaluate the home's condition. Mystified by the many blockades in the house, they immediately began to tear down all of the plywood partitions and walls. The home was then renovated in an attempt to capture her cotton-era grandeur.

By the end of the 1960s, a young couple employed by the school moved into the house at 12 Glebe Street. Both Scott and Rebecca Steinberg were newly appointed to the college's administration department. They were overjoyed at not only the proximity of their new quarters, but of its stately elegance. They took the second-floor master suite, the one facing out toward Glebe Street, as their bedroom. It was in this room that the Steinbergs realized why those protective walls had been erected so diligently years before. It was in this room that they realized the previous tenant was barricading herself from the ghost they saw one night in the late summer of 1968.

It was just a few minutes past nine o'clock at night when he made his first appearance to the Steinbergs. They were in bed, awake reading. The nightstand lamps on both sides of the bed were on, so the room was relatively well lit. He came and stood at the foot of their bed.

# THE COLLEGE OF CHARLESTON

The Steinbergs described the male ghost as being six feet tall and fairly well dressed. He wore a round-collared suit and a "fluffy" tie. He wore his hair cropped short. Scott Steinberg said the ghost reminded him "of the Victorian period." It was not the way he looked, however, that burned an indelible memory into the minds of both Scott and Rebecca Steinberg. It was what he attempted to do in that bedroom that made this sighting unforgettable.

The ghost began to speak. Rather, he tried desperately to speak. The couple said he looked almost directly at them and started moving his lips in a grotesque pantomime. No words came out of his mouth, just the moving lips of an ancient silent movie. After several seconds of this mute posturing, the couple both noticed a tangible look of frustration crest on the face of this long-dead young man. Flummoxed, he began to gesture with hands, furious to expel these very important words. After a moment of this, realizing defeat, he threw his hands down in frustration. He then put his eyes to the floor, disappointed, and departed. He left the room through a solid plaster wall.

As of this publication, the reason behind this post-mortem attempt at communication has yet to be discovered. The tax records, deeds and death certificates associated with 12 Glebe Street have not given up the answer as to the identity of this lingering spirit or his message. Until those clues rise to the top of this murky pond of a mystery, it remains unresolved.

The Glebe Street house is no longer a permanent residence. In the last few years, it has become the guesthouse for the president of the college, who lives next door in the Bishop Robert Smith House. There are no longer people in this house all year long to bear witness to this young man and his soundless attempt at speech. Does he still return to the foot of the empty bed in that front bedroom, desperately trying to converse with the pillows in the great theater of time? Or does he realize there are no living ears to hear his mute words and so remains unseen as well, hidden in the pine and plaster of the walls of 12 Glebe Street?

# THE OLD BICYCLE SHOP STACKING

There are many different ways for a formerly living being to manifest in this world. The living can see, hear or sometimes smell the validity of these beings' existence. In many cases, a severe drop in temperature can dimple the flesh of the witness as they stand within the bounds of the ghostly presence. Sometimes, for reasons left as mystery, a ghost cannot project these direct sensory guideposts, and becomes an obscure notation left for pondering and deciphering. Using philosophical reasoning, one can imagine a spiritual desperation to be recognized from beyond the grave. This is the case with the lingering spirit in a small nondescript brick building on the campus of the College of Charleston.

Built in 1965, the structure now houses the school's wellness center, a place for student healthcare. In simpler times, when the school was still mid-sized and sleepy, it was the college bookstore. With the college's incredible growth and popularity in the 1990s, they procured the larger old Sears Building one block away to use for the sale of textbooks.

For the first years of its existence, the building was home to Brauer's Bicycle Shop. The shop closed abruptly and tragically in 1971 when Mrs. Brauer was murdered in a botched robbery attempt. Her death signified the last chapter of this traditional mom and pop business, a final vestige from pre-cold war America.

When the building became college property in the early seventies, strange and unexplainable happenings began to occur almost right before the eyes of confused bookstore employees. The following describes what has transpired

multiple times throughout the seventies and eighties in this square building at 185 Calhoun Street. Many of the former employee recollections happened so long after the fact that the dates seem to blur and the frequency has become distorted. It can be chronicled that these events happened numerous times between 1972 and 1989.

Just before a new semester began, fresh textbooks arrived via truck. The bookstore staff prepared for the student onslaught—every book had to be out on the shelf in the proper section. Being a liberal arts school, the variety ranged from American literature to zoology, all with different professors and grade levels. It was not simple shelf stocking. It required detailed attention to a previously prepared grid.

After the shelves were stocked and the clock was punched, the store staff retired for the last hours of summer or Christmas break, depending upon the semester. Before they knew it, a stampede of disoriented and somewhat clueless college kids would descend on the little brick store to gird their scholastic loins with books, pens and astronomy charts.

Every blue moon, however, the carefully laid plans of collegiate retailers would unravel like an aged sweater caught on a nail. When the first staffers unlocked the doors an hour before opening one morning, their eyes fell upon a meticulously constructed vista that defied any explanation. All of the orderly shelving from the previous day's work was gone. In place were stacks—vertical stacks—of books. These towers, some five feet high, held neither rhyme nor reason. They had no scholastic order, just linear correctness. The harried bookstore employees, with precious few minutes before the doors opened, had very little time to ponder the insane pillars of paper. They could only work like automatons to throw things back in a state of order so the day's business would not be lost.

These towers of books, supernaturally stacked, are mystic arrowheads pointing to a long-gone corpus and a residual spiritual existence. The spirit of a woman slain in a spurt of violent, senseless greed still maintains residence in the old bicycle shop. She cannot be seen, smelled or heard. There are no variations in temperature to signify her presence on the floor of the building. These stacks—her own spiritual markers—point to her remnant energy in a vague, even obscure manner. These totems, made with building blocks of convenience, books with very little relation to her life, are the only way the deceased Mrs. Brauer can say: "I am here."

# MISS MARY VERSUS MOTHER NATURE

The house at 18 Montague Street in Charleston's oldest neighborhood, Harleston Village, has existed in many forms over the last two centuries. It is believed to have been one of the places President George Washington stopped during his spring 1791 visit. At that time, the new house was a luxurious urban villa. The original owner was an influential businessman and his home was a significant landmark in the borough. More recently, it has housed dozens of College of Charleston students. It is no longer a single-family residence, but has been chopped up into numerous apartments. It is through the senses of these transient residents that we have a description of the protective ghost in this once elegant home.

Wind and water have taken their toll on both the buildings and the people of this city. The deadly hurricane of 1813 exacted a terrific toll on the South Carolina coast. It was not as statistically powerful as other storms either before or after, yet in the arbitrary realm of natural disasters, that matters very little. The dynamics of her deadliness relied on the tides and the strategic placement of the storm's eye. Nearly twenty Charlestonians died and the shipping industry was battered into impotent uselessness for months. The storm also wreaked fatal havoc on the house at 18 Montague Street, a family and a faithful slave.

It came on a still and muggy August night. As the winds progressively rose, the whipping sounds became howls punctuated by crashing trees. From

inside 18 Montague, the Walters family and servants heard not only this cacophony, but also creaking noises not unlike a listing ship on a tempest-whipped sea. The family peered out of the windows until everything became a blur of gray. The father realized that the panes of leaded glass offered very little protection from the increasingly violent night. He yelled at his family and slaves to flee to the lowest level of the house, the servant quarters, a sparse brick room with a large fireplace for cooking.

The children screamed as the noises became louder and more intense. The sounds emanated from within, creating a sense of pressure that gave all of them the illusion that the house would be torn to pieces, hurling them into the swirling atrocity outside.

Miss Mary was the family housekeeper and nanny. The three girls regarded her as a mountain of protection. Her dark skin did not have any effect on their attitude toward the woman who reared them and listened to their most private fears and wild childhood ideas. Instinctively, it was her they gathered around. Their father shouted for them to get in the center of the room, in front of the fireplace. It seemed the safest spot. As long as Miss Mary was there, the little ones did not hesitate.

The strong woman did her best to calm her trembling charges. She enveloped them in her shawled arms and hummed calmly. She gave them all of the comfort she could muster under these conditions. In her sixty-six years, she had never heard the rain and the wind so angry. She was frightened herself, but knew she must never let the little ones see her fear.

In the midst of the chaos, everything froze. Then the entire kitchen quarter became a blur of noise and movement. The chimney began to crumble. Sections of brick fell from above onto the heads of Mary and the three girls. Without becoming frantic, she gathered the children closer and fell on top of them. Their muffled screams could not compare to the tumult of the bricks crashing and the breaking of the floor.

Miss Mary absorbed most of the falling bricks. Without a sound, she remained on top of the children, arms still outstretched, shielding them from the cascading bricks. Mr. Walters rushed over, nearly overcome with several direct hits to the skull, and shielded Mary and his girls from the few remaining bricks. It was over within a matter of seconds. Mr. Walters rolled Mary off of the girls. They immediately grabbed him, sobbing and gasping for air. The family then saw her face. It was serene and lifeless. She had stoically absorbed the falling bricks, saving the small children from an almost certain death. Walters put his hand on her forehead for a second, then he put his coat over her prone body.

# HAUNTED CHARLESTON

In 1988, College of Charleston junior Shari Oswald lived in a one-room studio apartment on the top floor of 18 Montague Street. Her first encounter with the ghost of Miss Mary happened on an early Friday evening in December. Shari was preparing to meet some friends for dinner. She was brushing her hair in front of a large vanity mirror when she saw, standing behind her, a very obvious and discernible form. It was an African American woman with a stoical, almost stern face. The woman wore a white bandana on her head and a loose, formless dress of the same color. Her hands were folded over her chest. She looked directly into the reflected face of Shari, nodded very subtly, then closed her eyes and turned. She disappeared into the wall of the apartment before the stunned Shari could turn, or even draw a breath.

Over the years, there have been incidents like this in different parts of 18 Montague Street. Most however have been in the upstairs studio apartment where Shari Oswald lived back in the late eighties. According to Dr. Evan Jones, current owner of the property, that room was once a small ballroom used during formal occasions. Almost certainly, Mary would have spent much time in that room, either tending to the regal houseguests at leisure, or quietly watching the three small children perform their clumsy dance maneuvers with each other. She would smile and watch as they pretended to be President Washington, or any number of the powder-wigged businessmen that came to see their father and attended his festive parties.

These girls are no longer children. They are now pockets of dust and buttons in one of the city's myriad graveyards, long since retired from this earth. Miss Mary still remains to watch out for them, to make sure that everything is all right for them.

# 1837 Bed and Breakfast

The 1837 Bed and Breakfast at 126 Wentworth Street is nestled in the great oaks of Harleston Village, just one block west of the College of Charleston campus. The house also serves as a home for the spirit of a nine-year-old enslaved boy named George. Guests have woken abruptly to the sharp sound of a bullwhip crack, only to be greeted with the acute aroma of hay and the impression of small feet on the end of their rice bed. On days when the air is totally still, this ghost is known to rock rocking chairs on the piazza. This ghost is one of Charleston's most playful, plying his mirthful mischief on unsuspecting guests. Yet his story is filled with saddened darkness, not of his making.

Sometime in the early 1830s, a contractor named Shilling found himself and his team of house builders employed to build a single house at 126 Wentworth Street. Among the deals worked out between Shilling and the owner of the property was that the family of one of Shilling's slaves would live and work at the new home for one year after completion. When the structure was finished, the owner, Mr. Holder, would have the option of buying the family.

When the house neared completion, George and his parents moved into the top-floor room closest to Wentworth Street. George was mainly used as a stable hand, washing down Mr. Holder's two brown thoroughbred stallions and feeding them daily. Occasionally Mr. Holder would send him on errands to shops not far away. George would go to the banks of the

Ashley River to play. He found great joy in watching other children, both white and black, frolic in the glassy water.

As time passed, Mr. Holder could no longer afford to keep George's mother and father. A rich planter from Virginia offered to buy them both for a high sum of money. A broker named Thomas Ryan was hired at a barracoon, or slave hotel, on Chalmers Street, Charleston's oldest and longest cobblestone road constructed of ballasts used on the high seas by ships returning from Europe.

Charleston was one of the great slave marts of the South. Sullivan's Island, on the north side of the harbor, is commonly referred to as the Ellis Island of African Americans because it was used as a large quarantine for the east coast slave trade. Two out of every five African Americans living in America today are believed to have descended from ancestors who first stepped foot on Sullivan's Island, South Carolina.

The city statesmen legislated for slavery and ministers of the Gospel upheld it as the best means of Christianizing Africa for the ultimate benefit of the whole human race. A score of men opened up offices downtown along State and Chalmers Streets in barracoons and dealt in the bodies and souls of men and women.

Most of the Southern owners of enslaved Africans never sold them. The enslaved were generally inherited from one generation to another. The workers on the various Charleston plantations such as Middleton and Drayton were the best physically cared for peasantry the world had ever seen. They were fed and clothed and their spiritual wants catered to. However, this class of property was subject to the same vicissitudes as all others and the cruel sale of slaves was necessary from time to time.

One of the remaining examples of a Charleston barracoon is 6 Chalmers Street—the "Old Slave Mart," as the inscription on the front of the building still reads—one in the same line of buildings where George's family was sold by Mr. Holder.

In many of the barracoons, the buyers interviewed the enslaved privately in booths, with the slave broker on hand. In public auctions, the enslaved men and women were advertised in the city paper three days before the auction. On the day of the bidding, the enslaved stood on a balcony, far enough away from the bidders so that no imperfections such as scars, cuts or gray hair were visible.

In the cellars below the barracoons along Chalmers and State Streets, bolts and staples have been found on the floors as well as manacles with chains for hands and feet. A barracoon was one of the cruelest fates for

the enslaved. Oftentimes a man would be in the cellar with the enslaved, playing a fiddle or mandolin to coerce the shackled men and women to dance about, strengthening their muscles and raising their spirits for the interviews and auctions.

One of the saddest things about slavery in Charleston, besides the blatant inhumane mental and emotional brutality of the practice, was that families were sometimes split up. The plantation slaves rarely worried about their families being divided because of the abundant wealth of their owners. However, downtown slaves were subject to the same economic woes of the townspeople.

Mr. Holder brought George's mother and father down to Chalmers Street to be interviewed in one of Mr. Ryan's brokering booths. George stood next to Mr. Holder's horse and watched silently through the open door of the barracoon. His parents demonstrated their various skills of weaving and cutting to the Virginia planter.

Within a short while, the Virginia planter shook both Mr. Ryan's and Mr. Holder's hands. A stack of paper cash and coins was exchanged between the three men and Mr. Holder leaned down to sign the bill of sale on the broker's desk. George's mother and father nodded over to George with tears as the Virginia planter escorted them out the back doors of the slave mart.

George was distraught over losing his parents. He had bad dreams of his parents being shackled and beaten. The night his parents were to leave he tossed in bed at these horrible visions until he awoke. George fled the safety of 126 Wentworth Street and ran toward King Street, the only way in or out of Charleston by land. There he hoped to catch up with his mother and father.

When George arrived on King Street, he began asking travelers how close he was to Virginia. A wayfarer lifted him up onto his wagon and let George ride in the back. George looked out the back of the wagon for hours, hoping to see his mother and father on the way to Virginia. His eyes eventually grew weary and he nodded off.

The next day, George found himself back in Charleston, alone in the cellar of a barracoon. His hands and feet were shackled. The door to the cellar opened and George could see that it was daytime as light poured in. Mr. Ryan walked in with Mr. Holder, holding a bullwhip. Mr. Ryan unshackled George and Mr. Holder threw the boy on his shoulder. George returned to 126 Wentworth Street to work in Mr. Holder's stable.

There are few records on George's life after the sale of his parents on Chalmers Street. Despite Charleston being known as the largest slave city

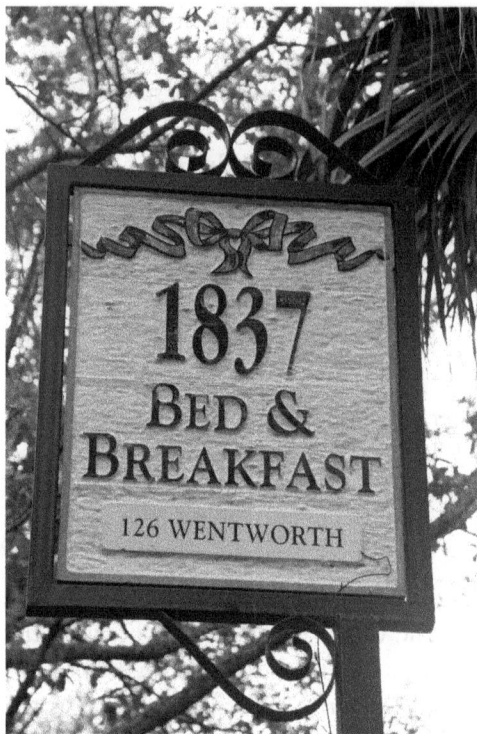

in America, slaves were not allowed to read or write—making family records virtually impossible to find. No record of the boy's death has ever been discovered. One theory passed down from the oral tradition suggests he may have drowned trying to swim out to the anchored slave ship where his parents were being held.

The 1837 Bed and Breakfast leaves guest diaries in every room. The two rooms and the balcony George and his parents resided in during the nineteenth century have had some unusual entries in these diaries over the years. In a small green suede diary, for instance, November 4, 2003, has two guests from Michigan, named Tom and Annie, recording their armoire doors and bathroom doors opening and closing throughout the night.

Earlier diary entries reveal more startling encounters with the uninvited guest. A woman from California named Maria penned an entry describing her experience during a hot day in June of 1999. Apparently the rocking chair outside her room kept rocking quickly back and forth, as if an energetic person was enjoying the rocker for the first time. Maria was trying to nap after a long day of walking in the still, hot air. She looked out the window and noticed that there was nobody in the rocking chair. Just at this time, the manager hollered upstairs, "Stop!" and the chair immediately stopped rocking. She asked the manager about this strange occurrence and the manager simply replied nonchalantly, "It's just George playing again."

On November 27, 1997, Dawn and Alex England from Naples, Florida, had the closest recorded encounter with the ghost of George. The Englands' diary entry reads:

# THE COLLEGE OF CHARLESTON

*Nov. 27 1997*

*Alex and I slept soundly in our warm rice bed all night after eating an enormous Thanksgiving meal of soul food and turkey at Jestine's Kitchen down the street. In the early morning, around six-thirty, both of us jumped up quickly in our bed when we heard the loud, sharp crack of a whip! Neither of us saw anything at first, but then there was barely morning light coming through the window and only a distant streetlight that we saw through the oak trees. I leaned over and turned on the lamp next to the bed and, as I did, we both began sniffing the room because of this overwhelming smell of hay! Alex mentioned the hay smell to me and I agreed. We began looking around the covers for hay grass and, as we did, we both stopped cold. At the end of our bed, at the back of both our covered feet, was the indention of two little feet! We both leaned over and we then felt the end of the bed quickly bounce! The impression of the feet was still there. We got out of bed and looked around but nothing else happened and the smell of hay quickly went away.*

While this ghost has yet to be seen, his youthful spirit and energy are all around the old slave quarters on the top floor of the single house. Despite the tragic ending of George's family, he still comes back to play in Charleston, at 126 Wentworth Street, today known as the 1837 Bed and Breakfast.

THE CITADEL

# GULLAH AND THE ORIGINS OF THE CITADEL

Montserrat, the great Caribbean volcano, created the 1822 "year of no spring" in Charleston. As warm air rose from lower latitudes, the Carolina skies clouded with lithic ash, enveloping the city in a perpetual eclipse. It was in this shadowy setting that Denmark Vesey and an African priest from Mozambique known as "Gullah Jack" Pritchard were accused of plotting a heinous slave revolution that would have killed every man, woman and child residing in the immediate area.

Trial records do not conclusively prove their guilt; they died denying involvement. However, on the testimony of two talkative slaves named Peter Poyas and Monday Gell, Denmark Vesey, Gullah Jack and thirty-three accused accomplices were hanged. The white men involved with the conspiracy were fined to a state of perpetual poverty, yet released. Hundreds of other co-conspirators were exported out of the Charleston city limits.

Down the street from the site of the executions is the city fortress built in response to Denmark Vesey and Gullah Jack's plan, The Citadel. The Military College of South Carolina exists today because of the alleged slave revolt of 1822.

Denmark Vesey came to America as a slave in the cabin of a vessel owned and captained by the man he took his last name from, Joseph Vesey. Captain Vesey bought the young slave in the 1780s. In his younger life, Denmark saw the successful Santo Domingo (what is now Haiti) slave revolution from the perspective of a man enslaved.

In this world of heat and anger, he would have seen firsthand the mysticism of voodoo, a blend of African religious beliefs and those of the myriad other cultures that merged in the name of planter wealth. Despite different shades of skin and tone of tongue, these humans were united by cruelty, bonded in the dark practices of the old world and their hatred of this new world.

Denmark Vesey won his freedom in his early thirties via the city lottery on King Street. The city lottery was designed to raise money for community needs. It's not clear exactly how Vesey obtained the winning ticket but, perhaps his master Joseph Vesey and he both bought the ticket with the understanding that Denmark would be given his freedom if the miracle of luck came their way. Denmark bought his freedom from Joseph Vesey in 1799 with the $1500 winning jackpot and lived fairly well off in his own house on Bull Street afterward.

However, Denmark was so bitter about having been a slave in his youth that he spent much of his time studying the Haitian revolution. He also emphasized the plight of the Israelites escaping Egyptian bondage in the Old Testament during his time as a lay reader in the African Methodist Episcopal Church on Calhoun Street.

Denmark Vesey was seen stopping slaves on street corners and preaching his view of the times to them. Six to nine thousand slaves were said to have enlisted in the revolt, which was to take place June 19, 1822, forty-three years before emancipation. It was also rumored that Vesey had coerced the Haitian government to come up to Charleston with militia in case reinforcement was needed. The revolt would have been the bloodiest in the dialogues of

American history, with every European-American man in Charleston killed, every women ravaged, and all the fortunes from Europe looted as the city smoldered in flames much like the French plantation houses during the successful Haitian revolt in 1804. For three months, the city militia and the revolutionaries knew of the June 19 deadline, while the average Charleston citizen went about their daily business, unaware of the ensuing mayhem that lay ahead underneath the ash-tainted spring skies.

The A.M.E. Church Vesey worshiped in, the second oldest in the world, was burnt to the ground, along with all A.M.E. churches in Charleston, in the city's state of paranoia after the alleged slave revolt, which was stopped on June 17. The free were outnumbered nearly three to one during the Vesey crisis. The A.M.E. church Vesey was suspected of having plotted his revolution in was rebuilt in 1867 and its tall steeple stands in review to the north of the old Citadel today. The burning of churches accelerated the racial tension in Charleston, as enslaved Africans took seat in the balconies of European-style churches. This balcony seating was the embryonic stages of the later Jim Crow laws of the 1920s that publicly segregated Charlestonians by skin color. Spiked ironwork guarded homes from intruders. Much of the ironwork was melted down to use as Confederate cannonballs during the Civil War, though it still encircles the tops of brick walls around a few downtown homes.

Gullah Jack was commonly referred to as a witch doctor. He embodied the secrets of voodoo mysticism. The witch doctor was known to bite the heads off of live chickens in ceremony. As the bird's warm blood flowed into his belly, he hoped to have visions of the supernatural. (One-hundred-and-five-degree fever from salmonella certainly must have induced visions of something.) Along with his beliefs in supernatural visions, Gullah Jack also believed that if he carried a blue crab claw between his teeth that it would make him an invisible ghost to the white man's bullets. He was hung with a crab claw between his teeth. Apparently, the arms of crustaceans don't protect against asphyxiation by hemp rope.

Gullah is an entire culture rendered from the bosom of Mother Africa, filtered through the Caribbean islands through slavery, then fused with an already hurly-burly mix of people in the South Carolina Lowcountry. It is a culture steeped in superstition—fascinating to those interested in the murky, more mysterious realms of the supernatural.

Minutes out of downtown Charleston finds the befuddled traveler on John's Island, South Carolina. The first confused turn down any dirt road will reveal homes—some no more than shanties—painted an alarming shade of blue. It is a rich, gaudy blue, like a handicapped parking sign. Ask a local what that color is and they will tell you "Dat's Haint Blue."

Haint blue is a color used by the Gullah culture of the Lowcountry to physically ward off the advances of haints, of course. If your confusion still lingers, a haint is a haunt, but a physical, half-living haunt like a zombie. Think of every stereotypical image of the Haitian undead; a wide-eyed catatonic stalker moving like an automaton, unaware of its surroundings. That is the easiest way to describe the somewhat amorphous haint, although several interpretations would describe it as more of a lost soul, like some of the ones discussed in this book.

There are connections to science in the engrained cultural superstitions of the Gullah people. Over the course of the last twenty-five years, experts in fields ranging from anthropology to ethnobotany have tried to explain the concept of haints. In the Lowcountry, these entities can be as capricious and vague as breezes blowing under the door or far more tangible and terrifying.

There have been medical investigations on the practice of zombification in the voodoo world that Gullah Jack is believed to have been influenced by. Whether he used these same voodoo practices in helping enlist fellow slaves during the revolt is unknown. However, he may have used the near-fatal toxins of strange fish and sea cucumbers to wipe on the arms of passers-by, only to enslave them later in a zombie-like state when he dug up their live comatose bodies from the ground days after they were mistakenly buried by grieving family members.

# HAUNTED CHARLESTON

Wade Davis, an ethnobotanist from Harvard University, went in search of the science to verify the reality behind the fantastical nightmare of the risen dead of the voodoo world. In his research, done in the 1980s, he concluded that voudon witch doctors used an ointment derived from exotic flora and grim, deceased fauna, to create a duplication of death undetectable by even modern Haitian medical authorities. The one ingredient in this balm that had true power and could create a metabolism lowered into death mimicry was the toxin of the fugu, or Japanese blowfish.

The possibility of meeting a person in this death-like state, or worse, being turned into an actual zombie, is the basis for spiritual protection at all costs among people of the Haitian culture. A stark blue color or quirky custom that might seem strange or tacky to the uninitiated visitor may be as serious as a pacemaker or open-heart surgery to the descendants of Gullah culture in Charleston.

You will see houses in and around Charleston, on hidden roads on John's Island for instance, with the shutters, or the front door, or maybe even the whole house, painted haint blue. There is an ancient symbolic quality to the color blue. The tomb of King David is shaded this color, and it predominates superstition in Islamic societies. Whether hanging as a bottle in a withered graveyard oak, or slathered on a poor man's front door, the color is believed to keep out evil, specifically determined as a haint or otherwise.

There is an old belief from across the Atlantic that evil will not cross over water; perhaps this shade of blue is representative of the eternal body of water. Ironic, considering that many in this culture are descended from people who came across the big ocean shackled in ships sailing on winds of greed and piloted by men blind to any good in humanity.

Though neither Denmark Vesey nor Gullah Jack's "haints" have ever been recorded, the Marion Square area where the old Citadel stands remains the eternal stalking grounds for two of history's most misunderstood figures that came across the Atlantic on those slave ships.

# The Lost Cadet

Amidst the regimented order that is the gray ranks of The Citadel dwells something entirely disordered and chaotic. Mingled in with the formality and discipline is an entity unaware of his rank or his place in this archaic class system. He is lost because he has been dead for nearly one hundred and fifty years.

Consider the tragedies and emotional tumult that have gone on inside the ramparted walls of The Military College of South Carolina. Many young men simply have not wanted to go into The Citadel, but were forced by their parents, people hoping to salvage a hopeless life by the rigors of discipline. Others could not wait for the order and the life of rank and file, only to find out they couldn't stand the personal attacks, the vitriol of plebian hazing. Some have gone mad with power, seeking not to instill discipline, but to frighten young men with violent threats and physical mayhem.

In 1822, in response to the threat of a slave revolution led by Denmark Vesey and Gullah Jack, the South Carolina legislature passed an "An Act to Establish a Competent Force to act as a Municipal Guard for the Protection of the City of Charleston and Vicinity." An arsenal and guardhouse was planned for the north end of Marion Square, and the building known as The Citadel—a Greek word meaning "fortress"—was erected.

In 1842, The South Carolina Military Academy was established at The Citadel and soon became known for its high academic standards and strict military discipline. By 1843, twenty cadets were enrolled in the new military college. Because of World War I and the increase in military enrollment, by

# THE CITADEL

1922 The Citadel had outgrown its old home and moved to its current location near Hampton Park.

To get to the cause of the phenomena of lost souls at The Citadel, we must look at the large number of suicides that have occurred on the grounds. They are of course kept low profile, but the press occasionally discovers them. Just recently, an incoming freshman leaped from a third floor balcony only moments after being dropped off by his parents. He was supposed to be headed to the induction ceremony. He was badly injured, but will live to ponder his actions. Others are not so lucky.

Hazing has always been an issue at The Citadel. In the 1980s, The Citadel refused to allow the filming of the movie version of 1967 Citadel graduate Pat Conroy's novel *The Lords of Discipline*, which created an intense debate about The Citadel's racial policies. A few years later an actual incident involving the hazing of a black cadet by fellow white cadets dressed as Ku Klux Klan members at The Citadel created a national sensation. This particular hazing incident was the first of many within the late '80s and '90s. In 1997, one cadet was dismissed and nine others punished for hazing and harassing two female cadets. That was only one year after females were admitted to the college.

The scenarios above, hazing and suicide, could be the reason behind the ghost that haunts the Embassy Suites Hotel on Meeting Street. This beautiful example of preservation was once the site of the original Citadel. After the school moved to its new location, the original building was almost fully abandoned for nearly seventy-five years. During those years, the city occupied offices on the ground floor for municipal engagements and a military museum. The building, eerie and dilapidated, was on its way to being condemned before the Hilton Hotels Corporation stepped in and negotiated a use for it with the city. The Hilton Corporation bought the old Citadel and soon reopened it as an Embassy Suites Hotel.

On the second floor of this fortress hotel exists an anachronistic, lingering spirit of a young man. Because of the unchanging style of uniforms at The Citadel, it would be difficult without a detailed investigation to determine from what century he hails. From numerous eyewitness accounts, many from hotel staff, he wears a gray jacket and stands approximately five feet six inches tall. The physical feature that has caused employees to quit and guests to check out in the middle of the night is hard to digest.

Every account of sightings in the hotel has one common denominator: the top of his head is missing. From varied descriptions, whether from stunned housekeepers or the Belgian cardiologist who encountered the figure in her room, it appears his skullcap was shaved off right above the brow. Although never described as gruesome, his visage is nonetheless disturbing.

# HAUNTED CHARLESTON

Dr. Anna Fletcher, a heart surgeon from Brussels, Belgium, saw the young man's ghost in her room in September 2003. It was just after three o'clock in the morning when she awoke suddenly. "I felt like someone was standing over me watching me sleep," she said. As her eyes began to focus in the dim room, she realized a young man in a gray coat was just five feet away looking at her. "He looked frightened. He looked like a cornered animal." She shot out of bed, clad only in her undergarments, and sprang for the door. She fully intended to run into the young man as she made her escape, but instead she moved right through his presence. She ran to the stairs and down to the front desk. She was given a robe and a ride to the Francis Marion Hotel next door, where she spent the last few hours of dark wide awake.

In a phone interview, she reflected on that night nine months earlier:

> Since it happened, I cannot get his face out of my mind. He was so frightened and confused, like he had just dropped out of the sky. Once I saw the shape of his head, I knew that he was . . . not alive. Seeing the image of a young man missing such an integral body part . . . I had to run. I could not comprehend it. I still cannot comprehend it.

The sightings have increased dramatically since the building became a hotel in the mid-nineties. This makes perfect sense. The building was nearly empty for many decades.

The ghost has not started making more appearances, it's simply that there are more potential eyewitnesses per square foot to see this young man, this lost cadet.

# THE GREEN LIGHT PHANTOM

A mysterious light that some called a spirit and others thought a hoax was a regular occurrence in First Battalion at the present Citadel campus, receiving statewide and national attention in 1981. The light first appeared as a dim glow to the two cadets living in room 1123 just before Thanksgiving of 1980.

But First Battalion has had reported sightings of ghosts since 1966 after a junior, who had been living in room 1423—exactly three floors above—plunged headfirst one night from the Fourth Division gallery to the First Division gallery concrete below. The Charlie Company classman, Will Hunter, was believed to have first come back as a ghost wandering between the B and C Company areas in the following years.

In the late 1960s, it was a superstition that only juniors could see the ghost. The spirit of Will Hunter was believed to have cursed room 1423. Another junior, Padgett Yarborough, who lived in that room four years later, died in a head-on car collision with a freshman cadet during their Christmas break, as reported by the November 17, 1972 issue of *The Brigadier*.

It is unclear whether Will Hunter or Padgett Yarborough was the ghost the two cadets saw in 1980. However, their stories seemed to disappear until a dim green light appeared to two roommates of 1123, Pat Finch and Bruce Sutton, in 1980.

The first experience with the dim glow was harrowing, according to one cadet. However, as the light appeared more frequently, the roommates got

used to it and invited others to view it. It first appeared hovering in the corner of the room near the cadets' presses, according to the cadet who woke and saw it first. He woke his roommate because the dim green glow was so bewildering. He wanted to be sure he was really seeing it. The glow did not disappear as the other cadet woke. The cadets discussed what to do about the light for several minutes before it slowly disintegrated.

After the Christmas break, the green light reappeared in the cadet's cold room at about 3:00 a.m. The light's intricate size allowed the cadets to warm up to it enough to stay in the same room with it. After the first sighting, the cadets in C Company became bolder and they woke others in the building to come and see it.

As others piled into the room, the small green glow did not disappear. One cadet flipped the light switch and the green light became dimmer, harder to see. The cadet turned the light back off and the men crowded underneath it, mesmerized. One cadet asked, "Who are you?" but the green light did not move.

Curious, the cadets asked more questions but the light did not respond until one questioner asked, "Are you a spirit?" Then he commanded, "Nod up and down if you are a spirit and side to side if you are not." The green light phantom moved up and down. Some of the cadets crowded to the back wall, away from the green light, while others filed quickly out the door.

The braver cadets remained in the room as word spread through the building that there was a ghost in the room of two men in Charlie Company. Sleepy cadets shuffled in the room, perplexed and weary of the phenomenon, as rounds of interrogations began. Several cadets, convinced the phantom was a hoax, stood on a chair and waved their hands through the green light to try and find where its source was.

The green light phantom revealed that it was a cadet. The series of yes–no questions revealed that it was a man who had been in C Company. The cadet had never graduated. Without a voice, the green light could not tell the name of his former self. As the cadets continued to ask more and more questions, the green light phantom eventually disappeared.

The roommates explained that the dim light made irregular appearances before Thanksgiving but "after Christmas Break it began to appear regularly." They stated that it had also increased in intensity and activity.

The light was reported nearly every night one cold week in February of 1981, bringing the interests of Lieutenant Colonel Daniel Cooke, The Citadel's public relations officer, three TAC officers and dozens of others to the room. One 1982 Citadel graduate who was interviewed about his viewing of the green light phantom had the following to say about it:

> *The light was similar to sheet lightening in that it was an area of dispersed light, and not a concentrated light source. The light would disappear from time to time and then, after several seconds the light would flash again . . . when it appeared the third time it seemed to be floating in mid-air, this time in the form of a concentrated sphere with the approximate diameter of a cigarette.*

In days before laser pens, this phenomenon was as creepy as it was perplexing. Many witnesses who communicated with the light believed it was a floating class ring, but when asked, the green light shook from side to side as if shaking its head.

The green light only appeared when everyone was off the floor, according to cadets. Theories were proposed about the possibility of laser holography and/or fiber optics as part of an elaborate hoax that was being played. Cadets looked around the walls of the room for some source but found none. Other men took off their shoes to see if the rubber of their soles was somehow grounding the light.

However, none of the theories disproved the dim green light. When the phantom made news in *The National Inquirer* that spring, it only added to the theory that it was a hoax. The occurrences in room 1123 eventually stopped in April of 1981. However, to this day nobody was ever able to disprove the existence of the green light phantom.

# PRESENCE IN THE
# FRANCIS MARION HOTEL

In the early thirties, when the Francis Marion Hotel was still new on the skyline of the Holy City, something grim happened on one of her towering floors. This incident could have been the result of the Great Depression and the tolling effect it had on middle-class America. Personal anguish, or the world's oldest setting for tragedy—the heart—could also have been the reason. Whatever the reasons behind this gruesome story, it has left a lingering presence in the venerable hotel. This spirit, trapped by decades of unfinished business, wanders through the corridors of the tenth floor in a purgatorial trance, gazing out over the lawns of the old Citadel.

A young man named Ned Cohen from Manhattan was in Charleston doing business for Florsheim Shoes. He volunteered for the business trip down to this steamy, remote city before anyone else had the opportunity to think about it. The company put him up in the Francis Marion, at the bustling intersection of King and Calhoun Streets, in the middle of the shopping district he was there to serve.

Cohen had an ulterior motive for coming to Charleston. He came not for the many retail merchants and department stores, but in search of lost love. A Charleston woman had stolen his heart one evening at a nightclub on West 32nd Street in Manhattan. This belle was only in town for a long weekend, but these two young people from different regions acquainted fast in the big ugly city. Passion grew within hours.

They had spent almost three full days together before Ned put in for a sales job to go to Charleston, according to Ned's employers and few friends

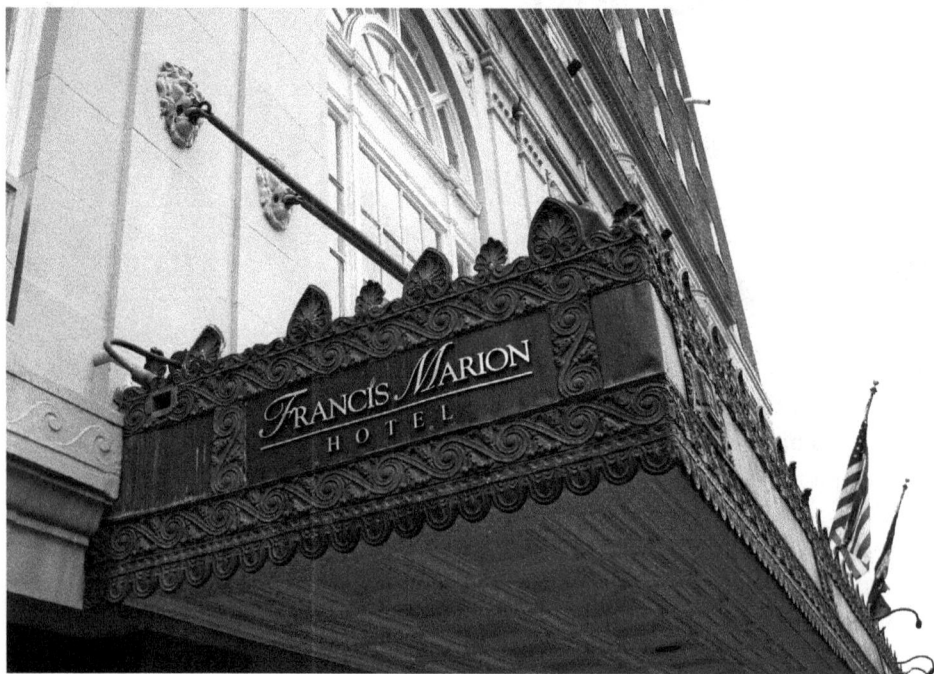

at Florsheim. He had called in sick for work with the flu, but his fever was for this Southern belle, a girl whose name is still unknown to these men who heard snippets of the brief affair from an unraveled Ned.

They know only that Ned found her in Charleston during his "business trip." She left Ned with a fatal note while he slumbered in his hotel bed: "I'm sorry. My family will never understand us. Good-Bye."

This unsigned note was found in the wool pocket of Ned Cohen's suit jacket hanging in the closet of his tenth-floor room. The large window in his room was wide open as the silk drapes blew in. His smashed body was found far below, face down in the middle of King Street across from the old Citadel.

The years leading up to this tragedy ranged from a spirited renaissance in America to bleak and miserable after the stock market crash on October 29, 1929. Black Tuesday, as it was called, left one out of every four Americans without jobs on Wednesday. Before the Depression caused by the stock market crash, changes in America had given people a surge of energy that sparked fresh ideas and new wealth.

In the 1920s, ragtime developed into jazz and young people flocked to dance halls and jazz clubs such as the one Ned found his *femme fatale* in. Inventions such as the gramophone and the crystal radio began to be mass marketed and instant music helped to popularize dance worldwide. Mad young people danced at home, at afternoon tea dances, in evening dance palaces and even later at nightclubs. Evening dresses suited fashionable dances such as the Shimmy, the Charleston and the Black Bottom.

Women were given suffrage and joined the commercial workforce across the country. World War I had reunited America, and the South was finally back on its feet after a long biter Civil War Reconstruction. Money poured into Charleston from federal government preservation grants and private donations. It was in these Roaring Twenties that the Francis Marion Hotel, filled with large crystal chandeliers and oriental carpet, was built to tower over Charleston.

After Black Tuesday, America became divided immediately into social classes based on economics. There were few who were not affected by Black Tuesday. Perhaps, Ned's Charleston woman was one of those few, having been reared into the inherited security of "old money" in the Holy City and embedded with its stoic ideologies.

In the days before forensics and toxicology, all assumed Ned Cohen had leapt to his death. He may have been drunk and stumbled while looking out over the city lights for his lover. Perhaps, he decided the best revenge for this

aristocratic damsel was to see his name and death report on the front pages of *The News & Courier*, knowing why he was there and why he had leapt.

The personal situation of Ned Cohen will never be known. His body lies in rest in a cemetery near Cooperstown, New York. But his soul, far from resting, wanders the eastern side of the Francis Marion to this day.

Occasionally, his presence has been felt in the chilling form of wind that suddenly opens up the window of his old hotel room on the tenth floor. Guests have been woken up by the window panes rattling quickly up, followed by the silk drapes, reported to slowly blow out onto the bed in the shape of reaching arms with thin hands, lightly touching horrified guests.

Ned Cohen also appears as a young man, suit jacket off, vacant stare on his face, wandering the halls. His face almost seems to question those who see him in the late evening hours, as if he is poised on the edge of a question. Perhaps he wants to know what he could have done to make himself acceptable in the eyes of the gentility down South. Perhaps he only wants to know the whereabouts of that beautiful young girl he met once in the cold asphalt jungle of Manhattan.

# THE HOLY CITY

# THE MEDICAL HAUNT

When Geoffrey Keith walked into his apartment on 140 Queen Street, he couldn't find the light. The smoothness of the wall next to the door startled him as he felt his way across the room. As he walked farther in, he noticed the furniture was misplaced as well. In the darkness, he stumbled toward the bathroom where he kept a night-light. As he entered the bathroom, he saw a white wax candle burning at approximately the same place where he kept the light. Geoffrey called out, worried of an intruder, as he walked back toward the open front door.

As a medical student, Geoffrey had seen enough grotesque, shock scenes of cadavers and illness that he was numb, for the most part, to fearing the dead. However, what Geoffrey saw in his apartment that evening in April 1987, sent him screaming down Queen Street and into his car. His extrasensory perception connected to the portal of a horrid, primitive operation in a dark room of one of Charleston's early hospitals.

The history of the Marlboro Apartments on Queen Street dates back to at least 1852. The building was originally Roper Hospital, one of the first downtown hospitals built, as Thomas Roper stated, "for the permanent reception or occasional relief of all such sick, maimed and diseased paupers as need surgical or medical aid." The building was a major progression from Charleston's original "pesthouse" built on Sullivan's Island in 1707 for patients with communicable diseases.

# THE HOLY CITY

The hospital was opened early in 1852 to combat a yellow fever epidemic and in 1856, two female nurses and two physicians were employed to allow the first regular patients to be admitted. There were originally thirty-eight regular patients, including eleven lunatics.

The hospital continued to operate, although not at all times smoothly, until the Civil War, when it became, in effect, a Confederate hospital. At one time the hospital was used to house Union prisoners of war. When Charleston was occupied by federal troops in 1865, the hospital and all its property was seized by the federal government and applied to its own uses. It was finally reopened in December of 1866.

Through one hundred years, Roper Hospital witnessed an earthquake, a tornado, several hurricanes, three major wars and innumerable financial crises for both America and the hospital. The original building was nearly condemned because of the great earthquake of 1886 that killed two patients and injured one hundred and twenty-five. In 1952, the old Roper Hospital was sold and converted into the Marlboro Apartment Building.

Geoffrey's account started with what he saw when he walked out of his bathroom in the dark that April evening. A low droning moan stopped him in his tracks as he looked back out toward the dim evening light seeping through his apartment's open front door. Geoffrey turned to his left and saw candles illuminating the grisly scene of a doctor amputating the leg of a dark-haired man in a blue military uniform.

There was no sound, save for the groans of the patient who lay sweating profusely while a dark, slightly translucent woman wiped down his wet, dirty forehead with a sponge. The doctor, whose face was not visible, wore a blood-splattered apron and used a crude saw to slowly grind away on the man's limb. Large, black leaches clung to the skin around the man's swollen, bloody knee. Geoffrey dared not look the ghostly physician, nurse or patient in the eye as he sprinted out of the Marlboro Apartments.

It didn't take long for word of Geoffrey Keith's chilling paranormal experience to circulate among the medical and scientific communities. Duke University, in Raleigh, North Carolina, received reports through their parapsychology laboratory. Unfortunately, the Marlboro Apartments were destroyed by the high winds and tidal surge of Hurricane Hugo two years later in the fall of 1989, before much investigation could take place.

Research reveals Roper Hospital's turbulent past over one hundred years; its physicians' records show seemingly archaic forms of treatment for patients with both physical conditions and mental disorders. Civil War soldiers had limbs hastily amputated to avoid fever and gangrene. The surgical tools used were so crude even a butcher would gawk. Patients with mental disorders were put in the insane asylum, a room brutally locked by an iron door with a peephole to look in and distribute food through. What Keith may have seen was some sort of portal into the primitive treatments and past conditions of the old hospital.

Historically, much of the documented paranormal phenomena from around the world seems intermingled with religious beliefs. The belief in the existence of miracles and other paranormal phenomena are staples of many Eastern religions, and even Western religious scriptures. The Old Testament is filled with examples of prophetic dreams and other paranormal phenomena. Individuals declared saints by the Roman Catholic Church provide some of the best-documented early reports of the supernatural.

Mediums offer the bridge between the religious world and science with the belief in spiritualism. The physical mediums—those who, while communicating with the dead, included physical effects such as the movement of objects, sourceless sounds and strange lights—remained the most popular. Harry Houdini, the great handcuff magician, spent a part of his life trying to disprove the work of mediums because he believed it interfered with the integrity of his own magic.

When the popularity of mediums began to die off in the early twentieth century, a new figure came along to rejuvenate scientific interest in the paranormal. This was Dr. Joseph Banks Rhine, who developed the Duke University parapsychology laboratory with his wife, Dr. Louis E. Rhine. By 1932, Rhine had demonstrated the existence of psychic phenomena (which he termed extrasensory perception, or ESP) through the use of card-guessing experiments. He was also able to show that ESP obeyed certain natural, psychological laws.

Many scientists and scholars have published their research to try and prove that humans can survive bodily death. Stephen E. Braude, a paranormal psychologist, published these words in the 2001 issue of the *International Journal of Parapsychology*:

> Some people believe that out-of-body experiences (OBEs) provide at least indirect support for the survival hypothesis. They claim that OBEs show that self, personality, or mind can operate from the body, which in turn shows that a human being is not merely a physical system. In that (so the argument goes), we have good reason to believe in survival of bodily death.

# THE HOLY CITY

Duke University's parapsychology studies of a person surviving bodily death leads one to ponder what it is to be without the human physical condition. A person, as a spirit only, would be unhindered by bodily movement and gravity, giving credence to the ethereal state of ghosts. A person's spirit, trapped in the theatre of time, would likely only be able to observe the physical world from the molded weightless impression of its former self. Without gravity, the soul would have an option of going anywhere, though some may choose to linger around familiar settings to try in vain to resolve unfinished business connected with mortal life.

Given parapsychological beliefs, Geoffrey Keith's extrasensory perception, or intuition, tuned in the scene of the medical haunt in the Marlboro Apartment Building that fateful spring night in 1987. But perhaps, if the amputee's spirit survived its bodily death, it was only tuning into the medical student to recreate his treacherous nineteenth-century night in Roper Hospital. With the aid of modern medical supplies many people today take for granted, this haunting may never have occurred.

# THE GRAY MAN
# REDUX

There are two types of ghosts discussed in this book. The first is the lost soul, a spirit not on this earth or in heaven. Perhaps this wandering entity is in the realm Catholicism calls Purgatory. Maybe they do not even realize that they are dead. They are products of tragedy, and Charleston buildings and thoroughfares run rife with them.

The other type would be called, by someone of faith, an angel. This is a mortal being, dead of this world and then borne up to heaven. Then, almost unthinkably, they return in spiritual form to this place because they love someone or something. They come back not to wander and wonder, but to deliver a message. In many recorded cases, this message is one of salvation. The Gray Man is one of those cases.

He was last reported seen in the third week of September 1989. James and Elena Cordray were strolling on the beach at Pawley's Island, some sixty miles up the coast from Charleston. It was dusk when they saw him: a gray man walking at their pace in the shin-deep surf. He can be called a man only because he took that very general human shape. Yet he bore no features, simply a shadow making his vague presence known to an unsuspecting young couple.

Despite his clouded anonymity, the Cordrays knew in a heart-stopping split second why he had shown himself to them. As residents of the island, they were privy to his warning. Even late summer renters know why he comes. His message is simple, sincere and deadly serious: "See me and leave. Now."

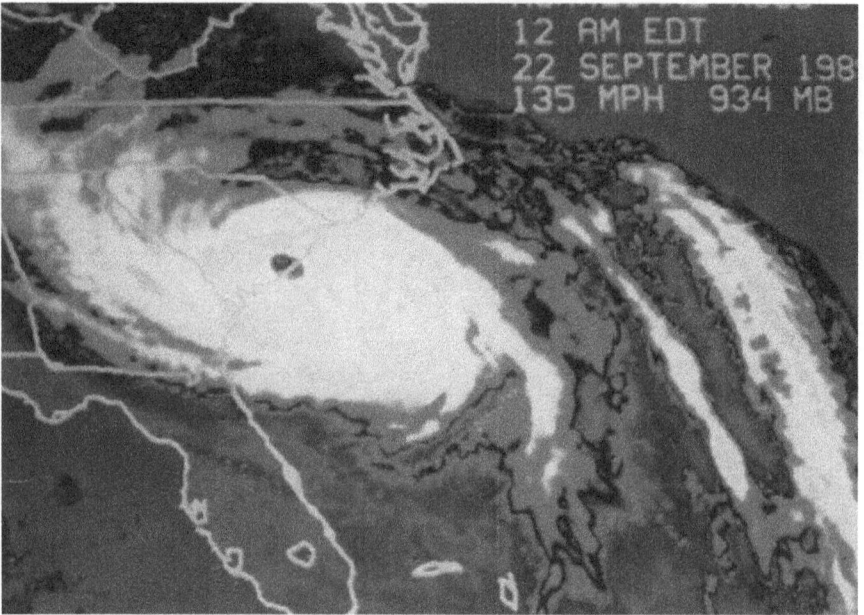

12 AM EDT
22 SEPTEMBER 198
135 MPH   934 MB

The Cordrays did just that. Without even a glance at their beloved home, they put their car toward the west and drove. They made a straight line to Kentucky, where they surprised some unsuspecting relatives.

To inland denizens and those who cannot smell the brine or plough mud from their yards, this may have seemed irrational, perhaps even insane. To people along the South Carolina coast, especially those who call Pawley's Island home, there really was no other alternative. They had to leave.

Hurricane Hugo obliterated the island south of the Grand Strand just fifty hours later.

Supernatural activity and Mother Nature hold the same shock value in South Carolina. Two great deadly earthquakes have plagued the coastline, one in 1698, the other in 1886, as well as thirty-three tropical systems. Every time a hurricane strikes, it becomes clear why the first indigenous tribes of Carolina never chose the maritime forests of the front beaches to settle.

The earliest hurricane known of in South Carolina was in 1600. Indigenous tribes passed on stories to the early colonists of the Charles Town area about the harbor rising up higher than the treetops the day the great storm came.

Scientists have been studying hurricanes in detail only for about a hundred years. South Carolina's history of hurricanes is one of the more expansive studies since the Mayans first named the huge storms "hurakans." The city of

# THE HOLY CITY

Charleston is brushed or hit at least once every five years, and has sustained a direct hit every fifteen to twenty years.

One of the most destructive tempests of Charleston's past occurred in 1752. The downtown area was nearly completely covered by the storm surge, and shifting winds pounded the area with tidal waves. Hundreds of people lost their lives in the violent hurricane, but its terror pales in comparison to the Tide of Death. This twenty-foot tidal surge killed nearly three thousand people in one night in 1893. The Tide of Death remains the deadliest in Charleston's history. Many islands went under water. Island houses, all built on wooden posts several feet above ground, caved down like card houses. Many collapsed, crushing their inmates on the spot; others drifted quickly off with men, women and children clinging to them. In the darkness of despair, Charleston residents clung to the swaying treetops of the giant pines and oaks until the roots gave way and together they were washed out to the reckless billows of the berserk ocean that had sent for them.

The ensuing days after the waters stilled were not very hopeful, especially for people just outside the more solid infrastructure of downtown. Nearly thirty thousand people were homeless. The island victims, with their clothing torn or completely washed away, wandered around naked looking for food and shelter. All vegetable growth was destroyed, all animals, even birds had been swept away and any fresh water was tainted with salt. The gaunt figure of famine drew near and stared the victims of the barrier islands of Charleston in the face.

Before the inventions of modern communication, coastal residents were given about four hours notice of a hurricane, if they were lucky. Mariners usually rushed in early from sea to warn port cities like Charleston along the coast. Technology saved thousands of lives when Hurricane Hugo roared over downtown on the fall equinox midnight of 1989. Hugo claimed seventy-six lives, half of those in South Carolina.

The storm fluctuated between its peaks of 160 mile-per-hour sustained winds over the Caribbean to the 138 mile-per-hour sustained winds that circled around its deadly eye when it made landfall. A sixteen- to twenty-foot tidal surge emptied the harbor of boats and demolished coastal property. The counter-clockwise motion of the storm winds and tidal surge wreaked the most havoc just north of Charleston.

In McClellanville, South Carolina, between Charleston and Pawley's Island, Lincoln High School opened its gymnasium to be used as a shelter. The gym was sixteen feet above sea level, the highest point in the area, and was built to withstand hurricane force winds. The structure withheld Hugo's fierce winds, but as the tidal surge covered the entire school, the water began to seep into the gym. The tide continued rising until people began swimming out of the windows and children were lifted into the rafters to keep from drowning. No one died that night, but everyone in the shelter was frightened to the core.

When James and Elena Cordray returned home four days later, they expected to find a suburban apocalypse. What they found instead, as they wheeled onto their cul-de-sac, destroyed their mutual concept of reality. Their Pawley's Island house stood unscathed among the flotsam and jetsam of what were once their neighbor's lives. Not only did it stand alone like a shining silver tower amidst the debris of chaos, but it stood secure and intact. Every shingle held stuck to the roofline. The French doors, left ajar in the couple's hasty exodus, left the home's innards naked to the beast wind. Yet every tiny detail—from china hanging in the cupboards to cartoons pastiched to the refrigerator with magnets—was untouched. If one is to believe the local Pawley's Island press, even a beach towel stayed hanging from the back deck facing the beach.

This is the legacy of the Gray Man that has existed in the consciousness of South Carolinians and in the lines of their lore for at least two hundred years. "If you are chosen to see me, then take the giant leap of faith and leave immediately. Both you and your property will be spared damnation from the storm."

With the weight of material possessions and sentimentality bearing down on them, not many people could make that decision and leave their homestead. Many have seen the Gray Man and could not leave, but only remark at the queer oddity that must have been an illusion illustrating a myth. It is this unfortunate group of skeptics and drunken boasters who die in the surge of glass shards and whipping, salty foam.

# THE STONE HOUSE

No other piece of real estate in the Lowcountry elicits widespread supernatural interest like the Stone House at 118 Folly Road on James Island. The home has gained a reputation over the years as a traditional haunted house, a den of poltergeist activities that scares new owners out and keeps it constantly on the market. It has become a legend in real estate circles. Many potential buyers have been scared away by the house's legacy, before even stepping foot on the property.

Built of heavy gray ballast stones back in the late 1920s by John Doran, the house looks like a traditional English home in the countryside. Doran was involved in the shipping industry, and would have had access to these great stones, once lined in the bellies of wooden ships. The house is stately and solid. But what lurks inside creates anything but a feeling of comfort for occupants.

Former residents have remarked on the abundance of ghostly occurrences that seem to infect this house from within. There is an area in the hallway that remains cold all the time, regardless of the time of year. Cold spots are common manifestations of a remaining spirit, sometimes making an isolated area forty degrees colder than the surrounding structure.

Residents have also reported seeing several embodied spirits in the house. There have been sightings of a small female child and the dim silhouette of a tall man. Another sighting was of a young woman with a flapper-style haircut from the Roaring Twenties. Residents and neighbors alike recall seeing ghosts mingling with the living during parties in the house. Ghost sightings are not the only manifestation in the Stone House. Several owners reported to *The Post & Courier* their smelling perfume, not light, but a quite heavy odor.

# THE HOLY CITY

Sometimes the ghosts in this house are proactive, offering assistance from beyond the grave. According to an October 28, 1991 *The Post & Courier* article, former owner Roland Cardwell recalled an incident during the Christmas season. His daughter had hidden a bicycle in the attic. While pondering how to sneak such a large and awkward gift downstairs, she went outside to get some smaller presents from her car. She heard a calamitous noise and rushed back into the empty house. The bike was standing on its kickstand on the first floor. The daughter thanked the helpful entity and left the house.

In a recent interview, one lifelong Charlestonian revealed actually seeing something from a moving car on Folly Road. At the time the house was vacant, with a "For Sale" sign standing near the busy highway. It was dark, and she was in the passenger seat of a car driven by a friend. As the vehicle passed the Stone House, she looked at it, as she had every time she went by. This time, however, blood-red light streamed from the attic windows. There was a shadowy figure in one of the windows, looking out at the headlights. The woman begged her friend to turn around. He complied, and they passed the house again. This time it was completely dark and empty, as a normal house should have been.

Theories abound as to who causes these inexplicable events or who these silhouetted figures might be on the property. One regards John Doran, the original owner and builder of the Stone House. People think he is watching over the property. Another story, never substantiated, involves a little girl who was struck by a car on Folly Road.

The stories will continue about this den of supernatural activity as long as The Stone House stands sentinel on Folly Road. Whatever causes these souls to wander the house is only overshadowed in fascination by the frequency of real estate signs on her front lawn.

# THE SECOND PRESBYTERIAN CHURCH

One sighting of the spirit in the Second Presbyterian churchyard took place back in November of 1979. Edwin Rose, a longtime member of the congregation, was helping to chaperone a sleepover for a youth group staying in the rectory building adjacent to the church. As dusk fell, he did a sweep among the headstones to make sure none of the children were still outside. As he walked back toward the northeast corner of the graves, he was stopped in his tracks by a solemn, illuminated figure.

The spirit was glowing from within, a white angelic light that stood out dramatically against the dark night in the Charleston churchyard.

Rose at first thought he was looking at the spirit of a woman. The figure wore a smock, seamless down to the tops of its feet, which Rose never saw. On the top of this entity's head was a pile of curls that hung to the jaw-line. But it was the magnificent glow that captivated Mr. Rose and caused him to freeze in the middle of the churchyard path. He could not bring his gaze from the intensity, and stared straight into it until the light dissolved into black.

Rose knew he had seen a ghost; there was no doubt about that. But being a dedicated member of Second Presbyterian and a fervent lover of history, Rose wanted to know exactly whom he had seen. He researched past figures from the church's last two centuries. Using the archives as his main resource, he uncovered a photograph of an old oil painting of a pastor with long, curly locks, like a woman, wearing a long robe—the Reverend Thomas Smyth.

Smyth was a nineteenth-century Scottish pastor of the Second Presbyterian Church. He regarded his role as pastor as the most significant job on God's

earth. Whether he was walking the streets doing his daily errands or standing in the pulpit of the church on Meeting Street, he wore the same garb. He wore the robes and powdered wig of Parliament. He dressed as barrister, considering the word of God to be the ultimate law.

Reverend Thomas Smyth is a remembered personality among the Presbyterians because of an enormous library of books he collected from Europe. He was knowledgeable and would use his skills to visit the sick for both spiritual and emotional intervention. Smyth left a lengthy volume of autobiographical notes, letters and reflections with his granddaughter, Louisa Stoney, that give clues about his life and spirit.

Frederick Adolphus Porcher, another Charlestonian, remembered Reverend Smyth as a bit of a chatter bug. Porcher says of Smyth:

> He was fond of talking and never let a subject pass him, but his talk was not always to the point. There was a great deal of palavering about him. All parsons are apt to get into a habit of wordiness from the necessity imposed upon them of frequent preachings. If they cannot provide a supply of thought, they substitute a large supply of words, and this was the case with Dr. Smyth.

The spirit of Reverend Smyth may have spoken his thoughts best by saying nothing at all to Rose that November night. But the spirit's appearance had inspired Rose to try and find out why Smyth's spirit sill lingered among the tombstones beside the church. Rose flipped through many pages of the church's history before reading through the letters and poems the pastor left in his volume of work with his granddaughter.

The Second Presbyterian Church was established in the early suburbs of downtown Charleston by mainly English, Scottish and Irish families. They adopted a then-respectable method of raising funds through a lottery. The congregation met and was formally organized on April 24, 1809, and elected Rev. Dr. Andrew Flinn, a native of Maryland and a strong Calvanist, as its first pastor.

The original congregation of thirty-one Presbyterians hired two brothers, James and John Gordon, bricklayers in their early twenties, to construct the sanctuary. The Gordon brothers' plans called for a steeple, but when costs reached $100,000, the church leaders had a low dome placed where the steeple was to have been. The church was completed in 1811, and Flinn preached the dedicatory sermon on April 3.

# HAUNTED CHARLESTON

The Second Presbyterian Church was originally nestled behind marshy tidal creeks right behind the Cooper River. Mariners called the church "Flinn's church" as they saw it through oak trees when passing across the harbor. As development continued in Charleston, landfill squeezed the church further from the harbor view. The church grounds are on the highest elevation of the old city area and have never been covered by the many hurricane tides that have inundated Charleston.

Flinn retired after only nine years and the next three pastors served only nine years all together. Reverend Thomas Smyth was the fifth pastor, but the longest-serving pastor the church ever had. He served as pastor for forty-two years and through the great American Civil War. During the Civil War, he donated the church bells to be recast as cannons. The bells were not replaced until 2004.

The stresses of the Civil War may have accelerated Smyth's age, and his later journal entries became fixed on his declining health, interlaced with reflections and conversations with ancestors. Certainly after laying down so many young men from the Civil War in his churchyard, and seeing his mortal days coming to an end, a morbid fascination with death must have begun to take its toll on the pastor. For forty-two years, the pastor harbored Presbyterian families with eternal places of rest next to his church until he took his quiet place among them in 1873.

The pastor caught what people around him considered "old man's disease," or what today would be referred to as Alzheimer's, after the Civil War years. His sermons remained eloquent and long, but the congregation was not always entirely sure whom he was speaking to. The pastor would seem to be talking gibberish to some, but to others he was beginning a sweet dialogue with the hidden dead relaxed in the grounds of the churchyard.

In his autobiographical notes and letters, Reverend Smyth wrote down a poem by the poet Southey as he was reflecting on his immortality in the afterlife. It's very likely the pastor recited these lines in his library next to the church.

> *My days among the dead are passed;*
> *Around me I behold,*
> *Where'er these casual eyes cast,*
> *The mighty minds of old:*
> *My never-failing friends are they,*
> *With whom I converse night and day.*

# THE HOLY CITY

*With them I take delight in weal,*
*And seek relief in wo:*
*And, while I understand and feel*
*How much to them I owe,*
*My cheeks have often been bedewed*
*With tears of thoughtful gratitude.*

*My thoughts are with the dead, with them*
*I live in long-past years,*
*Their virtues love, their faults condemn*
*Partake their hopes and fears,*
*And from their lessons seek and find*
*Instruction with an humble mind.*

*My hopes are with the dead, anon*
*My place with them will be;*
*And I with them will travel on*
*Through all futurity;*
*Yet leaving here a name, I trust,*
*Which will not perish in the dust.*

What Edwin Rose saw that November night in 1979 was the six-foot Scotsman who helped rear the Second Presbyterian Church with his dedication and perseverance. Because of his luminescence in the afterlife, many members of today's congregation believe him to be an angelic spirit; someone who has sacrificed a heavenly reward to tend to his flock, the people he knew and loved that once sat among the pews listening to God's word—not only his contemporaries, but their children and grandchildren and beyond. These people were his life, and he is still there among them.

# DRAYTON HALL'S PRODIGAL SPECTER

On a late summer excursion to Drayton Hall in 2000, world-renowned medium Elizabeth Baron saw four men hanging in the oak trees between the plantation house and the Ashley River. She said these men were put to death for not complying with the fever of rebellion during the Revolutionary War. William Henry Drayton had murdered these men.

While the clairvoyant witnessed the horrible scene of the men hanging, the specter of William Henry Drayton still roams the grounds of the plantation as well. He is the man that three people, including long-time docent Pat Parker, saw back in the 1980s peering from the upstairs window and walking down the avenue of oaks.

Drayton's image is not definable; there is no indication as to what era his clothing comes from. The men who hang from the oaks were seen wearing knickers and loose-fitting cotton tops characteristic of the late eighteenth century. It is believed that these men had questioned William Drayton's opposition to the Crown. Drayton's view on independence from Great Britain was a hard-line stance and these men must have crossed him during one of his passionate nights of insurgence.

What is known of Drayton is that this resentful prodigal died mysteriously and prematurely at thirty-seven in Philadelphia in the same year of his father's death. The inheritance of the plantation was passed over to his younger brother, and the frightening notion that William Henry Drayton returned after all the family members had died to reclaim his property, makes him the most obvious candidate for ghostdom on this regal barony.

Elizabeth Baron's work with the ghosts of Drayton Hall has received little rebuke because of her long-standing credibility as a medium. Her work is a form of spiritualism, which stems from the belief that living persons can communicate with the spirits of the dead, and that the human personality, in the form of a soul or spirit, survives bodily death. A mesmeric trance facilitates communication with the spirit world, giving Elizabeth Baron access to the past, and to Drayton Hall's prodigal specter.

William Henry Drayton was born in 1742; the son of John Drayton, builder of the magnificent plantation house on the Ashley River west of Charleston. William was the first Drayton son and was educated in England. He was a ne'er-do-well and a disappointment to his father, though he went on to prominent political fame as a congressman and obtained commercial success. Despite this, William never inherited the family manse, Drayton Hall.

As one walks across the lush green lawns of the plantation today, it is easy to drift back in time. In the years before the American Revolution, Drayton Hall was a hotbed of intrigue. Ardent supporters of independence gathered on these same lawns and in the plantation house and much of the planning for separation from the Crown was done here. These men voiced their differences with Great Britain in opposition to unjust taxes and resistance to high-handed royalty. Those who were not part of the rebellion were considered traitorous enemies and either executed or murdered.

Patriot and planter William Henry Drayton, like his father John, was greatly revered by Whigs on both sides of the Atlantic. He was very powerful and must have been exasperated that despite his near-brutal patriotism and his conviction to commercial success at any cost, he was not acknowledged by his own father. In addition, he was stripped of his inheritance because of his mysterious premature death in Philadelphia. His resentment is his unfinished business.

Some circles of historians have claimed that William Drayton died prematurely because of a weakened immune system caused by overworking. The man was known to engage fervently in meeting after meeting to ensure the success of the family plantation and his political career. He traveled extensively to link up with American Revolutionaries. However, even in the 1770s, the age of thirty-seven was considered the physical peak of most men's lives, making it difficult to believe that Drayton's energetic spirit and body would give way to sudden illness in his prime.

Only William Drayton and his closest colleagues know the true story of his death. Philadelphia was a hotbed for the festering troubles that culminated in the Revolutionary War and it is likely that Drayton had many enemies in the City of Brotherly Love. He could have been knocked off in a pistol duel and his friends might have sent word home that he had passed away suddenly of illness to save the family's face. His cause of death may have been much darker and secret with the death of his successful father occurring in the same year. William Drayton may have taken his own life, knowing his father's disappointment in him and suspecting his absence in the will.

Whatever the cause of William Drayton's mysterious premature death may be, his spirit still wanders on the old plantation, through the eyes of the witnesses he has been revealed to, lording over the manor and land he felt rightfully his since the years of the American Revolution.

# EPHEMERA

# THE RESURRECTION TREE

The exact age of this crape-myrtle tree is not known, but it predates many of the watershed disasters that have afflicted the Lowcountry. The tree was once a thick-trunked shade tree, gorgeous when it bloomed in the middle of a hot Charleston summer. It was a beautiful, silent sentinel standing duty as the parishioners of First Scots Presbyterian passed in to worship week after week. Shy little girls fawned beneath its boughs on Easter Sunday in their prettiest dresses, waiting for the service to be finished so they could indulge in the sweet confections back at home. The tree provided a backdrop for marriage and death, God's glory and Mother Nature's Fury.

It was just such fury that struck Charleston on a September morning in 1938 as a cyclone ripped across the peninsula from the Ashley River. It demolished the sheds in the City Market, killing over forty people. On its dreadful path of destruction and bloodshed, the twister scored one more beautiful, cherished victim. The crape myrtle was torn from the earth and left twisted on Meeting Street. After the human toll was mourned and the city looked toward rebuilding, some of the First Scots congregation planted the roots and the severed trunk of the old tree. Presbyterians, pessimists and goggle-eyed onlookers were flabbergasted when this ravaged remainder of a once-glorious tree bloomed again in the summer of 1939. It was truly a miracle!

No longer the shady greeter of summers past, the tree was now something of a conversation piece. Her old glory was replaced by a newfound amazement; "How can that tree that got flung down near to Tradd bloom?" Men pondered the tenacity of the tree, women looked skyward in thanks.

# EPHEMERA

Admiration grew for the tree as she turned toward her former fullness. Sixteen summers passed and saw the blooms emerge as spring faded into heat. She was just beginning to regain her post at the entrance to First Scots Presbyterian when Mother Nature's whim took the form of vengeance once again.

Three hurricanes, tornadic witches from the east, blasted Charleston in the 1950s. The adverse effects from the third, wicked Gracie, tore the bough off of the crape myrtle tree. Only a trunk remained, a shell to remind Charlestonians of their precarious position by the sea. The disheartened congregation again hauled the refuse of disaster from their small churchyard and grimaced as they passed the place where the favorite tree once stood.

Hearts and souls were lifted one spring day in the late fifties. A little boy walking with his mother one Sunday morning noticed it first. The branches were coming back! Would it bloom again? Once more, heads shook and smiled up at the heavens. By the summer of 1960, blooms perched on the ends of those branches, a salute to the more beneficent powers of Mother Nature.

Almost two decades of growth and renewal took place before a whole new generation of churchgoers. "One step forward, two steps back" may have been the story of this tree, but her secret motto was "Never say Die!" Mother Nature's decree was to say otherwise, though: In the winter of 1979, something that the Lowcountry rarely sees happened before our startled eyes. Old Man Winter bent down to kiss the Carolina coast. His frozen touch left an ice storm, the brand of weather Charleston people and Charleston trees have no inward defense against. The old crape myrtle tree, weakened by her past brushes with disaster, and used to the fair temperatures normally encountered here, passed away. Someone cut down the vacant trunk and filled in the stump with concrete to prevent the spread of rot, inevitable in death. Could it be? Could the stubborn old tree be gone? As one church member put it, "it took Jack Frost to finally kill 'er." She was gone, but not forgotten—not completely.

One fine Sunday in the spring of 1980, a young man, with his twin son and daughter, was marching into service. He recalled a similar day over twenty years earlier when he had shown his mama the branches of that tree that had "blown down." Daydreaming and squinting away from the bright April morning light, he now had to shade his eyes when his little daughter said, "Look daddy." He turned and saw, for the second time in his young life, something startling coming from the earth in that churchyard. From around the concrete tomb of the old stump, four new striplings were coming through the ground like the fuzzy horns on a doe. The roots still had life, and these feelers came searching skyward for sustenance and light.

The result is a tree that defies any sort of explanation. As the winds from Hurricane Hugo whipped through her branches, you could almost hear the tree scoff at the storm. She took the brunt of Hugo, as did the rest of the Lowcountry. The tree suffered as in the past, but in the last fifteen years has risen phoenix-like to stand post outside of First Scots Presbyterian. If history is a guide, she will stand until the Final Judgment. The circumstances behind this tree's existence may not be supernatural or paranormal, but are as amazing as the stories of the once-living that surround her still to this day.

# EXCAVATIONS: GRAVE SIGHTS AND QUICK COVER-UPS

Recently, the discounted dead in the Holy City have risen. The physical details of most of the corpses are unnerving and gruesome, as their mortal remains are on parade throughout the downtown area.

The city is embedded with curiously inscribed graves. While many dates and names appear amidst elaborate obelisks and tombs in the churchyards and cemeteries, the marked burials are only a partial census of Charleston's dead. On facts alone, there are estimated to be at least fifteen times as many people buried along the peninsula than those that actually had proper burials.

The latest excavations into the city's dark earth revealed the remains of a variety of castaway social classes. Slaves buried in oyster-shell layered pits, historic minority societies, potter's fields for the poor and unidentifiable and a misfortunate resident buried alive among a forgotten mariner's graveyard have all surfaced.

These former residents of Charleston were laid to rest underneath what are now the downtown area's thriving developments. The Medical University of South Carolina's Children's Research Institute, The Citadel's football stadium and two of the College of Charleston's public libraries have all had their grand openings delayed due to startling discoveries in these excavations.

The Medical University of South Carolina (MUSC) unearthed thirty-three Charleston-area residents from a potter's field in late 2001. The caskets date back to 1802. Records show that the site was one of Charleston's largest public burial grounds until 1825, when the federal government converted the

land for use as an arsenal, which the Confederacy occupied in November of 1860.

The area eventually became the Porter Military Academy (now Porter-Gaud School in West Ashley) in 1867 and was used as a parade ground and athletic field. MUSC purchased the site in 1963, and soon discovered over a hundred graves when they began construction on their basic science building in 1968. MUSC petitioned the city to remove the graves to a site on James Island, but no details of the removal or reburial have ever been found.

The site of the Children's Research Institute was a paved service area for the basic science building and parking lot before construction began in 2001. MUSC hired Brockington and Associates to do archival research and field investigations of the site.

Backhoe trenching in selected areas exhumed the remains of the thirty-three bodies, including at least one mother and her infant child. Ironically, most of all the bodies found on the site were children. The Charleston Orphan House sat several blocks away, and many of the dead children unearthed are believed to have been carried over from the orphanage infirmary to the public burial ground after a yellow fever outbreak in the early nineteenth century.

Markers and names were never found in the potter's field. In March of 2003, the remains of the bodies were re-interred within a hundred yards of where they were exhumed. A plaque near St. Luke's Chapel across from the new Children's Research Institute marks the new gravesite.

At The Citadel, the Military College of South Carolina, the game of football has always been a deep-seated tradition, though not always a winning tradition. However, the popularity of the downtown location for the Bulldogs' Johnson Hagood stadium prompted a major renovation in 2003, designed to attract enough people to host a commercial bowl game in 2006. The proposed new 35,000-seat bowl-game structure is planned in the hopes of selling tickets to 15,000 more football fans than the old stadium could hold.

At an earlier attempt at renovation in the mid-1990s, a startling discovery was made: the roaring crowds rooting at the top of their lungs for the pigskin had been cheering directly over a mariner's graveyard. The first crew of the *H.L. Hunley* submarine lay covered in silence with their broken coffins beneath the west stands stadium.

Restless spirits awoken from their peace in the disheveled graveyard would have ascended directly into the visitors' section bleachers. If the Bulldogs' scoreboard is any indicator, the ghosts' opposition to The Citadel's disrespect for the dead has been voiced loudly throughout the seasons since the stadium was built in 1948.

The most recent excavations of the graves beneath the stadium in the summer of 2004 brought to light many burial traditions and superstitions of the Lowcountry. Some coffins had viewing glass plates where faces might be seen. One set of remains was found with coins over eye sockets, a common practice designed to keep the eyes shut. Others had coins scattered across them, apparently to pay the toll to make it into the afterlife.

Except for one grave, the skeletons all lay flat on their backs, facing east. According to some beliefs, the directional placement of bodies is a Christian ritual allowing the dead to witness the second coming of Christ around the morning sun. However, the one exception—grave number 188—caused archeologists to halt their excavation.

The remains lay on the right, the skeleton slightly curled as if napping inside a wooden coffin. The horror of the body's position is that the person may have been ill or in a coma while being buried alive by mistake. The lack of proper medical treatments in nineteenth-century Charleston lends credence to the fate of the unremembered soul of grave 188.

Parts of the graveyard overlap with neighboring burial grounds. In some cases coffins were placed into burial pits that were dug years earlier, causing remains to co-mingle as they broke up in damp soil. It is believed that many enslaved Africans were buried in pits and then covered with oyster shells. Archeologists were able to tell what race the remains are after lab analyses.

Workers used small scraping tools when they arrived at the bones in the coffins. Bamboo and recycled chopsticks were used to scrape into the dry bones' mysteries. As bones were unearthed, they were placed in wooden caskets about the size of large crab pots. Anything of value was quickly removed.

Some graves were several feet deeper than others, indicating the lapse in decades between burials, or possibly gravediggers not wanting to dig too deep during a hot Charleston summer. The location of the burial grounds led Charleston historians to rejoice when archeologists found the original *H.L. Hunley* submarine crew.

The first of three *Hunley* crews drowned during a test mission in 1863. Their bodies swelled with saltwater inside the small, primitive submarine, making it impossible to pull the bodies out in one piece. The Confederates sent slaves down into the water to swim with hatchets through the narrow opening of the submarine. The slaves used the hatchets to hack the bloated crewmembers out. The remains were buried in the city's mariner–military graveyard. No accurate maps were available, but a construction crew finally found the *H.L. Hunley* crew underneath The Citadel Bulldogs' Johnson Hagood football field.

Charleston's older, other college, the College of Charleston, has had an even more expansive history of desecrated sacred grounds than The Citadel. Four cemeteries were uncovered as the College of Charleston razed the old Bishop England Catholic High School to make way for its new Addlestone Library in 2000. While the Catholic Diocese of Charleston is responsible for originally building over the four cemeteries, the college's fate of mistakenly desecrating the dead has haunted them ever since the 1960s, when they were suspected of building their last library on President Andrew Jackson's mother's gravesite.

President Andrew Jackson tried for forty-two years to find his mother's gravesite, which he knew was near the city limits of Charleston. Back in 1781, when she died of yellow fever that she contracted while nursing Revolutionary War heroes, the boundary line, known today as Calhoun Street, marked the city limits. Several years after the College of Charleston completed their former library in 1967, many historians determined that Mrs. Jackson's eternal place of rest was crushed underneath the college library on Calhoun Street.

A monument was placed next to the library as a great apology to her and the Jackson family, a sort of "Sorry, Mrs. Jackson," as locals refer to it. The monument reads:

*Near This Spot Is Buried*
*Elizabeth Jackson.*
*She Gave Her Life Cheerfully For*
*The Independence Of Her Country*

# EPHEMERA

*On An Unrecorded Date In Nov. 1781.*
*And To Her Son Andy This Advice:*
*"Andy, Never Tell A Lie*
*Nor Take What Is Not Your Own,*
*Nor Sue For Slander,*
*Settle Those Cases Yourself."*

The most significant detail about the monument is that it also serves as a grave marker. The first three words, "Near this spot," are another way of saying, "Egads! We just built the College of Charleston public library on President Andrew Jackson's mother!"

When the College of Charleston bought the old Bishop England Catholic High School from the Catholic Diocese of Charleston in 1998, they saw a great opportunity to build a better library on land surely clean-slated by Catholic confessions and prayer. Wrong again.

That the Brown Fellowship Society's cemetery had been there before Bishop England High School moved downtown in 1921 wasn't completely a secret. The Catholic Church bought the cemetery in the early twentieth century form the Brown Fellowship Society, a fraternal organization created in 1790 by five free African Americans as a social club looking for standing in society similar to Charleston's white aristocracy. They also provided funeral arrangements for their members. Many of the headstones in the cemetery had been moved to Cunnington cemetery and the Catholic diocese assumed the bodies had been relocated as well. However, the Brown Fellowship Society's superstition that disturbing the eternal rest of their dead could wake "haints," a Gullah word for haunts and spirits, kept their deceased underground. There are no records indicating that the old cemetery was ever moved.

There are many other known examples of cemeteries buried under the development of the city. For example, an old Presbyterian cemetery lies underneath the Canterbury House, a retirement home on Market Street, and the county parking garage behind the Mills House Hotel on Meeting Street is built over a Quaker burial ground dating back to the seventeenth century. However, the College of Charleston was startled to find not one, but four cemeteries underneath the Bishop England high school.

Soon after the Brown Fellowship Society's dead were discovered, the records of eight women and one man whose headstones were buried in a cemetery named Macphelah were discovered adjacent to the Brown Fellowship burial site. Broken grave markers and a brick burial crypt with human remains inside were found on the corner of Calhoun and Coming Streets as work crews prepared to move on with construction after a memorial service had been conducted for the Brown Fellowship Society's re-interred dead.

Coroner records from 1822 to 1868 show the names of three hundred and sixty people buried in Macphelah cemetery, including slaves and former slaves. Slave records are unusual in Charleston, but the recordings were a way to keep track of the many epidemics such as smallpox and yellow fever that have infected the town.

Site maps revealed two more cemeteries when the Macphelah cemetery was discovered. The Free Dark Men of Color, a society started by an African American rejected by the Brown Fellowship Society, was found to be directly next to the Brown site. The last cemetery discovered was that of the obscure but historic Plymouth Church. Both cemeteries were so old and disintegrated that few recognizable remains have been found during the excavation.

The Catholic Diocese of Charleston, in large part, paid for the excavation and research into the old cemeteries. Memorial services were conducted and family members were called upon to attend as a large monument was placed in front of the library to recognize the burial grounds. Though history cannot ever be changed, the College of Charleston and the Catholic Church took the opportunity to correct a great historic wrong and to redeem and preserve an integral part of Charleston's history.

While strolling across the campuses of The College of Charleston and two Citadel campuses, one should be aware that there is no safe haven from trespassing sacred ground. Or, in the case of forgotten grave sites, anywhere on the peninsula of Charleston.

# FUNERARY ART

The churchyards in the Holy City are repositories for some of the most unique and oldest examples of funerary art in the nation. Through these ancient pieces of stone, the modern visitor can channel the fear, the sadness, and the acceptance that came with death in this colony's earliest days. The following pages display some of the finest examples of these relics of the burial custom.

The following pictures are the work of local photographer Julie Scofield.

The skull and crossed femur bones symbolize death, which was an integral part of existence in the colony's early days. Memento Mori is Latin for "Remember Death." If one forgot about death in these early days of tribulation, one might also forget to pray for salvation. The death image reminded people to make the choice for eternal salvation rather than rot. *St. John's Lutheran Churchyard*

This seemingly broken tree, with a garland wreath draped over the jagged edge, is symbolic of "life cut short." The artisans purposefully created the severed appearance. *Unitarian Graveyard*

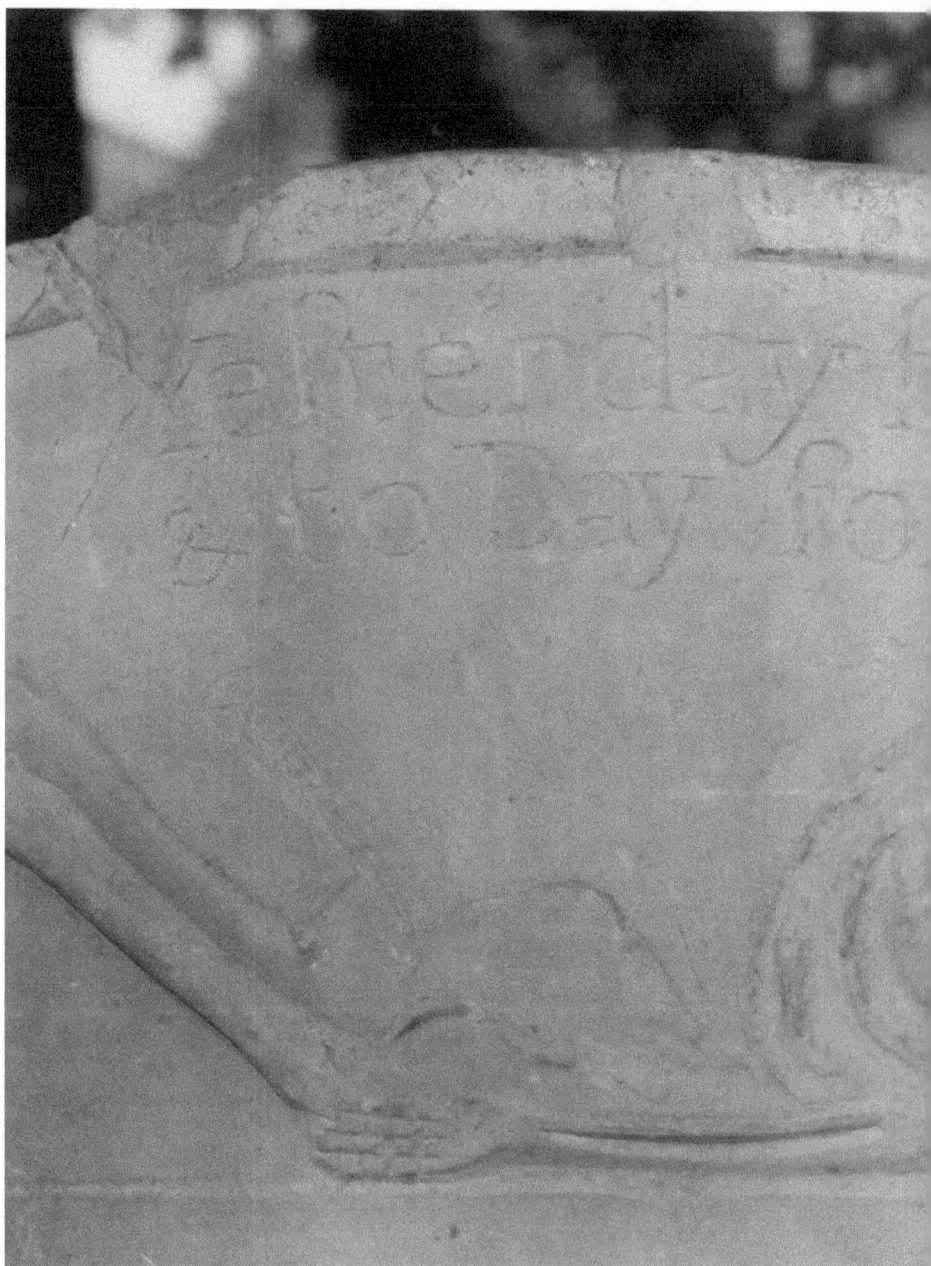

The gentleman buried beneath this stone was "cast off his ship on the sandbar" in March 1754. The image is the skeleton, that reminder of death, resting his skull on an hourglass with wings, the ultimate symbol of the passing of time and the brevity of our stay on earth. *West Side of St. Phillip's Churchyard*

This Death's Head from 1763 shows a little more optimism in the colonial outlook on death. The wings suggest ascension toward heaven, while the grinning skull represents the corpus. This was the early Puritan's way of not making a likeness of God, per the second commandment. *Circular Congregational Graveyard*

The grave artists would create a likeness of the deceased, either at the age of death, or as an innocent, cherubic youth. Ascension is shown here, with emphasis on humanity. *Circular Congregational Graveyard*

The engraving of the indigenous weeping willow tree on this grave marker represents the sorrow of a loved one lost. *St. Michael's Church Graveyard*

This tomb contains members of the Simmons Family, who perished in the mid 1680s. It is reputed to be the oldest grave in the City of Charleston. *Circular Congregational Graveyard*

All of these stones containing funerary art from the eighteenth and nineteenth centuries can be seen within a three-block area in downtown Charleston. If you visit these monuments to Lowcountry history, please do not lean on them or take rubbings from them.

These innocents play mirthfully amidst the symbols of ephemerality and death, while a visage of the deceased looks on. *Circular Congregational Graveyard*

The grave of Edwin Seabrook Mikell reads "A Favorite With All Who Knew Him. D. May 5, 1896." Mr. Mikell's Grave is one of the most spectacular in the entire city—but not merely for the craftsmanship behind it or the eloquence of epitaph. It has melded over the past century with this magnificent crape myrtle tree. It is truly a place of eternal rest. *Unitarian Graveyard*

# LAST WILL

When I was an undergraduate at the College of Charleston back in the final days of the 1980s, I lived and worked at a downtown funeral home. I really had no choice. My only other option was to live with my parents in the same room where I had "grown up." I gratefully resigned myself to the sights and smells of living among the dead. My quarters were a large room on the second floor. I shared a bathroom with another student named Tommy Cooper, who himself looked like a corpse that smoked far too much. Our rooms were just footsteps away from the technical sanctorum of the whole operation—the embalming room. The nauseatingly synthetic cherry smell of the glutaraldehyde sometimes made its way into our personal lives.

My job was to be on call from 6:00 p.m. until the secretary came in at around 7:30 the next morning, four nights a week. If a call were to come in, I would have to respond to it. By call, I mean the death call. This would be a hospital, nursing home or perhaps even a family member calling to request the services of my funereal overlords. I would put on my death clothes—a coat and tie, which could easily fall prey to an offending odor or stain in the night's work—and make the removal. I drove a 1985 Cadillac conversion coach, a long black hearse with a badass quadraphonic sound system and the permanent aroma of arranged flowers. I would drive through the deserted Charleston streets like a shaggy-haired grim reaper, glaring purposelessly ominous into each face that dared peek in. I would arrive at the morgue, or the old folks' home, or the suburban enclave, and efficiently and reverently put an expired human shell onto a uncooperative gurney, fill out the requisite paperwork, and remove the body to the funeral home in the midst of the Holy City's oldest neighborhood. Here the embalmer would work his art, his

# EPILOGUE

magic, his bread and butter. It was a gruesome task that ended with a waxy visage staring serenely back at us, despite the horrible contorted grimace that may have been there when we first met.

I had experienced hundreds of these nocturnal removals in my first year and a half of living in the funeral home, and it took an extraordinary distortion of the human shell to move me in any way: charred bodies, dismemberment and one described on the death certificate as "exsanguination due to evulsion of the thorax"—a junkie who had fallen between two moving trains.

For instance, one January removal still sticks out in my memory more than the rest. It was the only time I ever witnessed a post-mortem reflex, the "last gasp" as it were. It was a house call, at around 4:30 a.m. (they usually always were at an ungodly hour). The phone call was confused, a bit pissed off and the directions to the scene were sketchy at best. My cadaver-in-training roommate Cooper and I were to drive out to Wadmalaw Island. The dead gentleman was waiting for us in his hunting lodge.

The steel-belted radials of fate always put the hearse in the right direction, and true to form we pulled up, still legally asleep, at this nondescript wooden hut in the middle of what must have been an ancestral rice plantation. The rightful owners and generations of friends probably encountered many a loping buck just inside the surrounding thicket.

I met the son on the gravel driveway of this outpost. He had a face as grave as the heart attack his father had just had. He turned out to be a no-nonsense

# LAST WILL

South of Broad attorney, the kind of man who probably incessantly bitched about too many tourists gawking at his home. He motioned for Tommy and I to follow him into one room of the place. It was that cave all hunters convene in after a day of ticks and windburn, where guns went up on the wall and soaked duck boots were left by the buck stove to dry out for the next day's venture. There was a card table set up against the far wall, next to one of those miniature refrigerators normal college freshman have in their first dorm rooms. Seated at this card table was the deceased. He was garbed in khaki and a button-down, more L.L. Bean than Red Man. He was in his seventies, bald, and of regal stock; a blueblood, from aristocratic lines running down past the trunk of Reconstruction into the roots of the Confederacy. I found out later when I faxed his obituary to the paper that he was descended from an officer who rowed General Beauregard's ultimatum out to Major Anderson on Fort Sumter in 1861. A true hero in the ancient sense, but this man's current repose bore none of the dignity of his forefather's bold deed.

He was propped up on one elbow. His fingers were clutching a red and silver Bud Light can, literally warmed by the hand of death. His face was staring down at the table. He was stopped cold in his tracks by some internal explosion or implosion, stiff as frozen poultry seated at that card table. Tommy and I knew his family must leave the room while we put the body on our board with the gray fake-fur cover. It would not be easy battling rigor mortis in a daze of dreamy fatigue. The stern survivors left after one final farewell. This would be the last time they would see this man in a natural state, if frozen in death with a beer in one hand could be considered natural.

When they left the room to talk about a future without the patriarch, Tommy and I began our tricky task. Tommy, being the obscene gallows humorist that he was, pretended to take a swig out of this man's last beer. He was perfect for this job, I thought, and has since gone on to become a funeral director. I took the man's torso from under the shoulders, while Tommy gathered up his lower body at the knees. We nodded at each other, lifted up and removed him from his seat. His body remained in a stubborn fetal position on the board on the floor, like an old man crouching to protect his loins from an attacker's kicks. We could not roll our precious cargo past the family in this condition. It would be a huge distorted lump, not the flat discreet package we prided ourselves on carrying away. We must straighten this man out; make him lie down for his exit, this all-important moment during the removal when grieving kin saw the company's first example of professionalism and handiwork. Tommy and I worked in a series of tacit nods and hand gestures. We did not want to let on that there might be a snag, a flaw in the gears of funerary custom. He would lie down for us.

# EPILOGUE

We took our respective places at either end, pushing down like two manic masseuses, determined to knead the kinks out of our overworked client. As Tommy's bony frame sat on the dead man's legs, I pushed on his shoulders and chest. He came undone, so to speak. He began to comply with our desperate ministrations, but this man would not go gently into that long dark Cadillac. I was absolutely unprepared for the sound that suddenly emanated from the dead man's mouth. It was a rumble that built to a quick and very final crescendo. It sounded like a kielbasa and beer belch, recorded and then played backward at a slower, malevolent speed. It was demonic. It came from the bowels of hell, or at the very least, the bowels of this man who had been dead for nearly two and a half hours. What was this abominable noise that caused two veteran corpse handlers to pale in the middle of a shotgun shack out in the boondocks? Was it all of the ghosts of this man's privileged past coming out to exist with the deer and the squirrels on the land once maintained by tortured souls plucked from a riverbank in the middle of a similar African boondocks? Was it evil manifesting itself into the lives of two poor college students just trying to do their jobs? Or was it this man's final breath, trapped in his diaphragm, released from the shell of his body by us straightening him out? That seemed the easiest explanation to swallow. We had experienced a phenomenon that until now had been legend, the story told to separate the men from boys in this business, the tale told to scare the shit out of the effeminate hairdressers who sometimes came to the funeral home to put the finishing touches on the old blue-haired dames who had been faithful clients in life, and still, in death.

Whenever I stroll along the Battery and gaze out at Fort Sumter, I think about many things. I think about the many sleepless nights in 1860 had by officers and politicians on both sides. I think about how scared those bastards in blue must have been when that first shell exploded over that pitch-black fort on that April morning in 1861. I think about the apocalyptic legacy—the burned cities, the legless grizzled men in those sepia-toned daguerreotypes, six hundred thousand bodies, all American, all dead. If you walked across the battlefield at Gettysburg in July of 1863, they say you could get to the other side without actually touching the soil; the dead were strewn like thick flesh carpet.

I also think about that brave, genteel officer rowing out to that fortress on a sandbar to tell the Yankees, "leave or else all hell is going to break loose." And that noise, that sound I heard in the woods on that January morning, when I was young and quite dumb.

EBM 2004

# SELECTED BIBLIOGRAPHY

BOOKS

City of Charleston. *Centennial Proceedings: Charleston Orphan House.* Charleston: Walker, Evans & Cogswell, 1891.

Davis, Wade. *The Serpent and the Rainbow.* New York: Simon & Schuster, 1985.

Elgison, Howard. *The Unholy City: An Irreverent Romp Through American History Featuring Charleston, South Carolina.* Charleston: J.P. Rowell Printing, 1990.

Fraser, Walter J. *Charleston! Charleston !: The History of a Southern City.* Columbia: University of South Carolina Press, 1989.

Greene, Harlan and James L. Hutchinson. *Renaissance in Charleston: Art and Life in the Carolina Low Country, 1900–1940.* Athens: University of Georgia Press, 2003.

Keith-Lucas, Alan A. *A Legacy of Caring: the Charleston Orphan House 1790–1990.* Charleston: Wyrick and Company, 1991.

King, Susan L. *History and Records of the Charleston Orphan House.* Columbia: SCMAR, 1984.

McKnight, Gene. *The Charleston Orphan House, 1790–1951.* Charleston: Gene McKnight, 1990.

Pearson, Edward A. *Designs Against Charleston: The Trial Record of the Denmark Vesey Slave Conspiracy of 1822.* Chapel Hill: University of North Carolina, 1999.

# SELECTED BIBLIOGRAPHY

Smyth, Thomas. *Autobiographical Notes, Letters, And Reflections of Reverend Thomas Smyth*. Charleston: Williams, Cogswell, and Evans, 1910.

South Carolina Historical Society. *Charleston Alone Among The Cities*. Charleston: Arcadia Publishing, 2000.

Strangstad, Lynette. *A Graveyard Preservation Primer*. Walnut Creek, California: AltaMira Press, 1995.

Walker, Lois A. and Susan P. Silverman. *A Documented History of Gullah Jack Pritchard and the Denmark Vesey Slave Insurrection of 1822*. Lewiston New York: The Edwin Mellen Press, 2000.


## ARTICLES


Bellaccico, Bradley. "The Curse of "C" Company." *The Brigadier*. Charleston: The Citadel Board of Publications, November 17, 1972.

Braude, Stephen. "Out of Body Experiences and Survival of Death" *International Journal of Parapsychology* 7, no. 1 (2001).

"Graves Found at College Site to be Honored." *The Post and Courier*. January 25, 2001.

Gunnells, Charlene. "College Construction Uncovers 4 Cemeteries." *The Post and Courier*. March 24, 2001.

———. "Coroners' Records Lead to New Questions About Remains." *The Post and Courier*. January 26, 2001.

———. "Remains from MUSC Site to be Reburied with Service" *The Post and Courier*. March 21, 2003.

Kropf, Schuyler. "Grave Excavations Tell Tales of Past Traditions." *The Post and Courier*. June 29, 2004.

Langley, Lynne. "Archeologists Find Old Graves at MUSC Children's Institute Site." *The Post and Courier*. December 14, 2001.

Parker, Penny. "Haunted House?" *The Post and Courier*. October 28, 1991.

Von Lehe, Diedreich. "Ghost Haunts C Company?" *The Brigadier*. Charleston: The Citadel Board of Publications, February 20, 1981.

# ABOUT THE AUTHORS

ED MACY, a native of Charleston, South Carolina, has spoken about ghosts on CNN, The History Channel, HGTV and Fox, as well as other media networks. He graduated from the College of Charleston with a master's in English.

GEORDIE BUXTON is a native of James Island, South Carolina. He has guided tours on foot through the historic district with TourCharleston, LLC, and Supernatural Charleston, LLC, as well as by boat in the Charleston Harbor with Sandlapper Tours. Information on Buxton's tours is available at www. walksinhistory.com. He is the author of five books: *Channel Surf*, *Haunted Charleston*, *Haunted Harbor*, *Haunted Plantations* and *James Island*.

Photographer and owner of Red Room Studio, GLENNA MCKENZIE was born and raised in Charleston, South Carolina. She travels worldwide capturing weddings and following her passion for street photography. Trained in photography with a strong graphic design background, her unique view and techniques pull the viewer into the moment.

Red Room Studio was opened in 2006, and Glenna has been capturing weddings professionally since 2000. The business continues to grow and excels because of excellent quality, personalized service and Glenna's passion for photography.

Please visit us at
www.historypress.net

www.ingramcontent.com/pod-product-compliance
Lightning Source LLC
Chambersburg PA
CBHW060754100426
42813CB00004B/811